Me, Myself, My Team

How To Become an Effective Team Player Using NLP

Angus McLeod, PhD

Revised edition

Crown House Publishing Limited
www.crownhouse.co.uk

First published by

Crown House Publishing Ltd
Crown Buildings, Bancyfelin, Carmarthen, Wales, SA33 5ND, UK
www.crownhouse.co.uk

and

Crown House Publishing Company LLC
6 Trowbridge Drive, Suite 5, Bethel, CT 06801-2858, USA
www.CHPUS.com

First published 2000. Reprinted 2001. Revised edition 2006.

British Library Cataloguing-in-Publication Data
A catalogue entry for this book is available
from the British Library.

10-digit ISBN 1845900340
13-digit ISBN 978-184590034-2

LCCN 2006932137

Mixed Sources
Product group from well-managed
forests and other controlled sources
www.fsc.org Cert no. TT-TOC-2082
© 1996 Forest Stewardship Council
FSC

Printed and bound in the UK by
Cromwell Press, Trowbridge

This second edition is dedicated to Salli G
A friend in deed

About the author

Angus McLeod was an academic research scientist responsible for day-to-day leadership of significant, externally funded projects before moving into industry, where he held a number of roles, first in technical management, including quality, then in marketing and sales. He moved into general management, including COO and chairmanship jobs, before taking up consultancy. His most recent corporate career was in the environmental sector.

He has held numerous commercial directorships and continues to sit on a number of company boards, mostly in the environmental or training-and-development sectors. His business experience includes a buy-in MBO for an international financial institution (Perpetual). His consultancy experience in the last ten years has developed into leadership, team development, coaching and mentoring. He and his colleagues offer facilitation, course design, and training in a multitude of management and leadership skills, as well as providing coaching, mentoring and supporting consultancy for growth and change.

Dr McLeod is widely published in leading journals in the USA and UK, where his business is primarily directed. As well as this book, he wrote the widely acclaimed *Performance Coaching – The Handbook for Managers, HR Professionals and Coaches* (2003), which is the practical resource book featuring real coaching situations and dialogues. He designed the thirteen-day Diploma-Course in Performance Coaching for Newcastle College with more than 7,000 student registrations in its first year (2004) and assisted in the development of standards in coaching and mentoring for the UK (ENTO, 2005). He travels widely and regularly contributes at conferences around the world.

McLeod co-founded the Coaching Foundation Ltd in the late 1990s – a not-for-profit organisation helping to develop best practice in coaching and exposing the membership to a wide range of new thinking. He also runs personal-development courses – including

'Question of Balance', 'Wellbeing from Healthy Thinking' and 'Write-One', a writing course – in a number of countries.

He was the inventor of and motivator for Ask Max, the Internet-based e-mentoring service, which has been available since 1999 via his organisation, Angus McLeod Associates.

McLeod has bachelor and doctoral degrees and is trained in NLP and co-counselling. He has a diploma in performance coaching, is one of only a handful of Master Meta-Coaches in the world and a member of the International Society of Neuro-Semantics. He is a full member of the Neuro-Linguistic Psychotherapy Counselling Association.

He is a keen motorcyclist, involved in training to an advanced level. He is also a competitive rower and passionate cook. He works from Philadelphia in the US and from the West Midlands in the UK.

ourinfo@angusmcleod.com
www.angusmcleod.com
www.coachingfoundation.org.uk

Contents

Acknowledgements

I am grateful to April Curtis, who opened up her Raleigh, NC, home and office. She provided me with everything necessary for a writer. I am eternally grateful to her for her hospitality and friendship. I want to thank Lex McKee for the mind map, Salli G of Nutty Tart Grafix for the illustrations, and, last but not least, my warm thanks, appreciation and love to Obie Watson, who provided great support and encouragement in the final stages of the first edition.

I wish to thank Clare, Caroline and David at Crown House for adopting this second edition and for their successful work in bringing *Me, Myself, My Team* to a truly international audience. My thanks and appreciation to you all.

Preface

If you will, imagine two managers sitting next to each other at a business meeting. They share many similarities in background, education, skills, training and commitment. One is startlingly more effective than the other. What are the secret ingredients that make the difference?

Arising from all your competencies and everything you do is the difference you make as an individual. Add to that individuality the secret ingredients and you have startling individual performance. This book is the recipe for that difference, and there are two broad areas of cuisine. The first is *flexible thinking* and the second is *openness to self-challenge*. It is these, more than anything else, that make the performance difference: from good to startlingly effective. Put a Team together using these skills and two plus two equals ten!

The science of emotional intelligence tells us that to improve our management of others we need to start with greater self-awareness. This, then, needs to be followed by actions that manage self differently. This mental exploration and the experiences that we have tend to raise awareness of the similarities and differences between self and others, with new and fascinating perceptions. And when all these new abilities are mastered we experiment and improve our ability to influence/manage others. For that reason, there are practical explorations and information here about the different ways in which people are stimulated to action.

Throughout this book, I use the word *Team* with a capital T. This Team is what you define as: a small project group, a departmental Team, a group of divisional managers or CEOs.

Although the book is structured in form, I have destructured the content so that some elements of the skills are touched on before and after they are introduced. This should make some of the read-ing familiar and increase the recall that my readers have for the content.

Angus McLeod
Worcester

Introduction

When I first made the move from academia into industry, I reinvented myself as a go-getting, success-at-any-cost manager. I was bright and self-assured and got things done. People who got in the way of my vision (of the corporate goals) were manoeuvred out. I was operating from a set of ideas and beliefs that, although apparently successful, ignored the benefits that come from real teamwork, or the 'two plus two equals five' phenomenon. What changed me was the catalyst of pain. I rose fast and was cut down twice, in each case my patterns and competencies being out-matched by more politically agile people. With hindsight, it would have been smarter not to fail but instead to make the essential changes in thinking performance for myself. The two essential traits necessary for that to happen are openness (to challenge and new ideas) and flexible thinking – it is not necessary to fail in order to learn!

Each of us is already gifted with phenomenal ability. And some of that ability is invariably trapped in set ideas and beliefs that limit our perception and the chance to perform superbly. The keys to releasing our abilities are those two traits: openness (to challenge and new ideas) and flexible thinking. This book is designed to develop openness and flexibility by offering you and your col-leagues a set of tools that may be used to create your own change and success both as an individual and as a Team achiever. The first part of this book investigates the similarities/differences that we have in relation to other people. Then we explore those further to consider the similarities and differences that you have with your Team as a means of introducing some of the flexible-thinking skills that will be used throughout the book. It may be useful to read quickly through Chapter Three (whether you have a current Team or not) and complete the working examples. The book is designed as a working manual and reference work, which refers both back-wards and forwards to other work and working examples.

Much of the thinking behind the book comes from current practice and ideas in coaching, learning science, neuro-linguistic programming

(NLP) and coaching. My premise is that individuals operate internally as Teams. For example, I am a leader in directing and compelling myself to take business risks, but there is another part of me (my internal 'follower') that is fearful of doing this! And there may be 'Team communication' going on in my head: 'Go for it!' and 'That's too risky!'

This approach opens up new perceptions and learning for both the person and the Team in which he works. I would further argue that, unless each person has a properly functioning and efficient Internal Team, his performance in real Teams is questionable. My aim in sharing this book is to address the Internal Team and extend that thinking into the real (External) Team. The process is one that encourages both flexible thinking and also unique and individual solutions for each reader. My belief is that readers are more compelled to work through their own solutions than to borrow a standard 'system' from management theory. The best answers will be your own. It is part of this thinking that I bring to my work as a coach in business, catalysing individuals to fly. With luck, the receiving Teams will also embrace this work, and the beating of individual wings will be in harmony, allowing the Team to soar beyond the limitations of other Teams. In my experience, any change in one person leads to change within the Team. Even if only one person is flying, others will quietly practise and adapt themselves for flight! Enough of metaphor! The premise I make is that 'culture' is the result of similar behaviours, but it grows by the dynamics of similarity/difference.

The skills in this book enable you to have more choice about where you have similarity or difference with your Team (or a desired Team that you aspire to work within). When you change your behaviours they create change around you. Where others match this in the Team, you have a changed culture. Matching behaviours constitute Team culture. Your effort can therefore help the success of your organisation and is measurable by you. You can do this by noticing the changes that happen around you and whether or not these changes are in harmony with your own choice of behaviours.

We begin, then, by looking at the similarities and differences that we have when compared with others.

Chapter One

Thinking Preferences

Summary

We think differently and are motivated differently from other people. Only when we understand our own thinking can we make choices about a particular strategy to use in a particular situation. And understanding our own thinking processes leads to realisations about the differences between ourselves and others. These realisations lead to choice and the potential for improved communication, impact, influence and Team performance.

This chapter examines thinking preferences in order to give you insight into your own thinking preferences and how other people are similar to or different from you. It should also provide you with 'reasons' for how some people behave and why they may be effective or dysfunctional in a Team at the moment. Understanding creates opportunity for development and improved performance.

Understanding thinking preferences

Many of us tend to be surprised when other people do not understand something as easily as we do ourselves, or when they fail to grasp fully the importance of an issue. Most often, we project our own thinking preferences onto other people and assume that if they don't 'get it' it's because *they* have a problem. Let's stop right there! We cannot force change on someone else (without their full willingness and participation); it is a hopeless and wasteful task. So let's start with a set of beliefs that are empowering and enabling for you in the Team. Buying into these fully will give you a greater chance of success within all Teams.

- I cannot change what other people do, but I can change what I do.

1

- People have different thinking styles and preferences.
- If I understand other people's thinking styles and preferences, I can communicate with greater impact.
- I am responsible for getting my message across; it is not the receiver's responsibility.
- The better I communicate with colleagues, the greater our combined productivity.
- Understanding leads to trust.

Now let's look at some different kinds of thinking preferences. (I have drawn on NLP, learning theory and psychometric personality methods, including LAB profiling (Charvet, 1997) in setting these out, as well as aspects taken from my book *Slay that Dragon*.) The list below is not definitive. There are many ways to categorise understanding of people and their preferences. This list offers some insights as to how other people prefer information, how they use it and how they make decisions. The process is illuminating – whether accurate or not – and the benefits for you and your Team are considerable.

Left- and right-brain preference

The concept of *left and right brains* is one of the simplest and most widely known models of human psychology. It was brought to general attention (see, for example, Erdmann, Hubel and Stover, 2000) in 1981, when Roger Sperry shared the Nobel Prize in neurology. He asserted that our cognitive processes are largely split into mental activities on the left or right side of the brain. Thus, logical processing, comparing, organisation, structuring and arithmetic are all thought to be activities that predominate in the left brain. The right brain is concerned with emotional expression, creative inspiration and play. It may be assumed that the commercial, Western world is mainly populated by people with more left-brain skills than right-brain skills. Likewise, we can expect to find more instinct, inspiration and creativity in the East. As Sperry said at the Nobel ceremony, 'The great pleasure and feeling in my right brain is more than my left brain can find the words to tell you.'

Whether correct or not, it is easy to imagine that there are people who have dominating intelligence on one 'side' of the brain rather than the other. In the USA and Europe there are many working people who are attracted to organisations that operate in logical, left-brain ways. This can occasionally mean that the Teams are perhaps weaker in emotional intelligence, intuitive solutions, creative explorations or the ability to 'play'. It can be very challenging to those with left-brain thinking preference to 'let go', to play and run with the experience. It is only a preference and a determination to improve right-brain skills will result in raised competence in creative thought and intuition. Activities that stimulate the right brain include reading literature and self-questioning: 'What is my gut feeling?' for example. We can also encourage the right brain by opening up to creative expression through art, play and instinctive writing, for example, poetry written directly onto the page without editing during the creative process.

In the fast, changing world of business more managers need to be flexible and creative in their thinking and behaviours. Many managers are locked into reactive firefighting rather than the careful creation of strategy. Stimulating right-brain activity has to be a good way to encourage more flexible thought and creativity. These lead us to new inspirations, new possibilities, more effective strategies and methods.

The right-brain-dominant thinker can enter into a state, similar to trance, called *psychological flow* (about 20 per cent of the population are able to do this), in which words, images and/or feelings flow out and any structuring is left to subconscious processing, free of logical thought. Tim Gallwey (2000) calls this state, 'Self 2 focus'. For example, right-brain writers do very little thinking – they just write and edit afterwards. During the creative flow they create structures (associated in the left brain) as a *subconscious* support to their right-brain creativity. When the creative flow has ended, the writer discovers (cognitive, left-brain logic) that their work is already very well structured.

The state of 'flow' can be so captivating that the person will not notice people speaking to him. This can create problems if the trait is not understood and overtly discussed with those who may be affected by it.

Creativity is not of course isolated in right-brain-preference thinkers. Left-brain-preference people also have variable levels of right-brain aptitudes.

The state of 'flow' can be so captivating that the person will not notice people speaking to him.

Where a person is right-brain-dominant, he may be weaker in project managing and can be more inclined to tweak and adjust rather than complete tasks. Again, these are just preferences and determined efforts will improve their left-brain skills. They can also challenge themselves by asking logical, objective questions that invite mental processing. These are likely to include 'how' and 'why' questions: 'Why did I finish that report late again?'; 'How can I create a plan that will get my next report completed on time?'

If you wish to influence left-brain thinkers, then logical argument is likely to be the key (but read on, because other preferences can also modify these preferences). In contrast, the right-brain thinker may be more interested in the 'what' and easily bored by the 'how' – this too is influenced by other preferences.

Visual preference

Visual preference

Visual preference, *visual representation* and *visual intelligence* are some of the names given to the intelligent storage, processing and recall of visual images. People who have a highly developed visual preference may be in jobs that use their skills, such as design engineering and graphic art. Another clue to visual preference lies in the language that our colleagues are using:

- I see.
- I can picture what you are saying.
- This looks good for us.
- There's light at the end of the tunnel.
- I'll keep an eye on the situation.

Noticing language can help us to communicate more effectively with a person in the Team. Using visual language and charts would be a preferred way of introducing information to a colleague with a strong visual preference. Also, if that colleague has produced reports and presentations, it might be worth looking at the way *they* prefer to communicate so that, if you wish to influence them, you mimic their communication preferences. Because these are preferences, your efforts are rewarded because the colleague will be more alert and stimulated – they will not have to struggle to understand your key messages. Here is part of a report that would appeal to someone with a rich visual preference:

> Quarter 2 provisional figures show that Quarter 3 results (see diagram) may be below target. The picture is not complete. Our partnership with Fall Inc. during Quarter 2 has led to falling transport costs and the savings have not yet appeared in the P+L accounts. The chart below shows how costs have tumbled from Week 9 (Quarter 2). These savings will influence the Quarter 3 figures very significantly, catapulting Quarter 3 by 4% NPBT. I see us hitting the Quarter 3 target.

There are visual words such as *see, view* and *picture*, and the phrases invite a visual reader to make mental pictures, e.g. 'I see us hitting the Quarter 3 target', 'catapulting Quarter 3' and so on. The text is supported by diagrams and charts, too. Visual-preference readers do not just read the report: the text itself triggers the creation of pictures in their minds. They are stimulated because of the writing style.

Auditory preference

Auditory preference

If you recall a Team event or meeting and ask your colleagues to summarise their experience of that in ten individual words, you may find a colleague who uses a number of *auditory* words. Here is a selection of phrases containing auditory language:

- I hear what you say.
- Sounds good to me.
- That went with a bang.
- I'd say that …

Speech is the preferred method of receiving information for auditory people, but reading may also appeal. When an auditory-preference person reads, he is likely to 'hear' what he is reading – an auditory stimulation.

Where a colleague is highly auditory, he may prefer to get oral reports rather than written, and may be quite happy doing most of his communicating on the telephone. If you have to write to a colleague with an auditory preference, then using language that invites the reader to hear will be more stimulating for him. For example:

> I met with Joanne this morning. She said, 'Rachel, the interconnects are failing. Something needs to be done.' We discussed the quality reports and it sounds quite bad. Briggs and Company do not seem to have heard what we have been telling them as regards quality. I attach highlights of our copy letters and faxes. I propose that you speak to them. You have the ear of the chairman and your inter-vention may achieve more than our grumbles about quality have, lower down the organisation.

Kinaesthetic preference

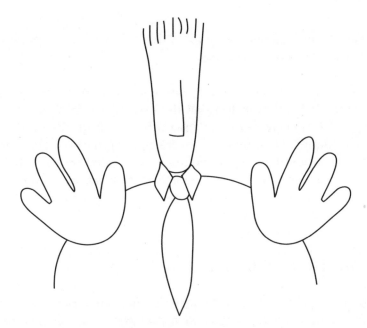

Kinaesthetic preference

For some people, the physical and feeling dimension is important in storing, processing and retrieving information. In other words, they are *kinaesthetically stimulated*. Indeed, their actions may be made on the basis of feeling rather than logical, or left-brain, think-ing. A highly logical person might find this frustrating – just as the kinaesthetic person is likely to be frustrated by logic that ignores their own feelings.

The phrases that someone with a highly evolved kinaesthetic preference may use, include:

- I'm going with my gut on this one.
- My sense is that we are onto something.
- I feel out of touch with this project.
- Let's hammer this out once and for all.
- I'll sniff out the competition.

The touchy-feely language does not necessarily link with a thoughtful, kind or sensitive disposition. Many of our most strident leaders of businesses act on 'gut instinct' while trampling over people in their path!

Rachel's note to someone with a high kinaesthetic preference might read something like this:

> Joanne and I touched on the quality issue with the interconnects this morning. We both feel that the issue needs forceful action. Briggs & Company have been insensitive to our quality concerns and, as things stand, these issues are going to hurt our customer relations. Could I encourage you to make a move on our behalf? You have a special relationship with their chairman and your physical intervention with him may succeed in stimulating action where our feeble attempts have failed!

Linguistic preference

A high level of linguistic preference manifests in a person's accessing information by reading[1] and a preference for writing things down.[2] Note that another reason for writing may be a dislike for personal contact! Information may be rather clinical, or it may be

---

[1] However, photographic recall is an aspect of visual preference.
[2] The stimulus may be complicated, since writing with a pencil or pen can stimulate a kinaesthetic preference also.

devoid of experiential character. I remember hearing of a communication that was written by a colleague to a Swedish company and included the line, 'I feel that we should ...' The reply contained the memorable line, 'We fail to comprehend why you bring feelings into the situation ...' Linguistic-preference people may be quite turned off by feelings – stick to the facts!

Interpersonal preference

This demonstrates itself most easily in those who seem always to get what they want from you in spite of your best intentions. The gift of the gab, compelling conversation, attentive listening are all components. People with a highly developed interpersonal preference prefer face-to-face interaction above all else. Having a highly developed interest in people does not ensure that they will act in order to satisfy you. They may be manipulative because they know how to do it and a few will enjoy the outcome of that. They can also be very supportive and kind. They may dislike formal written communication, preferring face-to-face and telephone conversations.

Creative preference

Innovative people are not just logically questioning and self-challenging, but they add another dimension that, as we have seen, is usually associated with right-brain activity. Almost certainly, creative preference is further expressed in ways that satisfy several other preferences and styles. Creative people are turned on by fresh approaches and thinking. They are easily bored by procedures and the systematic, detailed development of ideas. They tend to like choice in how they do things and options when having to follow procedures. Many are attracted to computer technology, but you can anticipate a problem if they dislike procedures and documenting their work! The journey of exploration itself is often more rewarding than making notes about the process and sometimes the journey is so interesting that they are not stimulated to finish, preferring to adapt and adjust again and again.

Systematic/procedural preference

This preference is exhibited by people who need to access information sequentially from A to Z. Going off track in order to illustrate a point unsettles them. Each step must be followed by the next without elaboration. Information prepared for the systematic or procedural preference individual needs to be prepared with the question 'What next?' continuously in mind. This helps keep a logical focus and assists the reader to assimilate the information quickly. Tables are especially attractive to procedural-preference readers. Many will be confused if you do not explain steps logically.

Unfortunately, the stepwise process can be frustrating for people who do not share this preference. The skills of system and procedure are vital in organisations. However frustrating the type may be to others, we need to understand that the Team may fail without them.

Numerical preference

Numbers people should be excellent in this domain. If it is possible to express information in figures, then this will be appealing for them. Often they will be turned off by vague argument and gut feelings.

Away-from and towards preferences

Look at the list below and identify those actions that are motivated by an urge to move *away from* something and those that are motivated by a desire to move *towards* something.

- We did that before so we will not make that mistake again.
- The targets are set at 6 per cent ahead of budget for the forthcoming fiscal year.
- That's the third accident in that car. I'm not having green again!
- I aim to double our sales turnover within three years.

When creating arguments for a group of people it is important to include both types of language.

When preparing proposals for managers who have a *towards preference*, you need to highlight the *positive*. There may be pitfalls that need to be detailed in a proposal for them, but not like this:

> Buying Acme will get us out of our uncomfortable position on stock holding.

This is an away-from sentence. To appeal to a towards preference we need to focus on something positive in the future. The above might be better written:

> This acquisition will positively impact on our desire to reduce our group stock assets.

It's often the case that senior people in bigger companies have a strong towards preference. If you are reporting into that level and wish to join the Team, your language will need to reflect that. These preferences are among the most *consciously observed* by many people in management. Most people run both patterns in different contexts but often have a tendency towards one or the other. When you are creating arguments for a group of people, it is important to include both types of language.

Big-picture and detailed-picture preference

Big-picture and detailed-picture preference

Many people are aware of this preference consciously. Details bore the big-picture person. The detailed-picture person often cannot understand information coming from the big-picture person because it is too sketchy. Here, then, is a great Team challenge: how to satisfy all the people all the time! One component of this may be to use *introductory summaries* in presentations and reports rather than summaries at the end. The summary should give just enough context to allow detailed-picture people to get a hold of the idea before reading on. Big-picture people probably will not read on unless the presentation appeals greatly to their other preferences! Details can be grouped together as bullet points or placed in tables and figures. Summary information also needs to be clearly identified so it can be easily recognised, without your having to hunt for it.

Past, in-time and future preferences

I am a very *in-time* or *now*-focused person. So I find people who keep referring to the past (the 'don't-mention-the-war' syndrome) very frustrating. By contrast, future-preference people have so much investment in the future that they do not necessarily complete the present. By the same token, people with an in-time preference may also demonstrate an inability to complete work, since their effort may be directed at the newest task rather than work in progress. The consequences can be remarkable. An executive in one company I led would lose everything in his in-tray below the top sheet. Unsigned letters could be found there weeks later. If his desk was cluttered, he would work only with what was visible and forget everything below.

People with an in-time preference may demonstrate an inability to complete work.

Understanding the time preferences of colleagues can assist you in using language that appeals to them. It is a fact that management decisions are best made in the present. For past-preference people, past experiences will be important factors in motivating (or not motivating) action. Future-preference people will be motivated by contextual information about consequences in the future. If you do not know the preferences, then you need to embrace both extremes to get support for a decision. It is also clear that, for good decisions to be made, a mix of preferences in the Team is vital. Sacking large proportions of older staff leaves a major weakness in organisations. The older workforce are the ones with enough experience to be able to focus on the past and flag up potential problems without having to reinvent old mistakes and challenges. Where a mix of preferences exists in the Team, all three preferences need to be catered for in communications. Here is an example of that:

> Our shareholders are demanding a higher rate of acquisition and three are already well advanced now. These have an estimated total capitalisation of 3.2 billion. Our new goal must be twice this level in two years and our experience suggests that our hit rate is 30% with an average lead time of 21 months. The forecast suggests that we may hit 1.2–2.3 billion by the end of the current fiscal year. Experience also tells us that the lead time and success rates are 50% better in amenable regulatory markets. We therefore propose that we immediately reopen prospects in both our domestic markets and in the UK. To achieve our goals we must look for three potential corporations at about 1 billion each. The board has formed a new acquisition Team under Alan and Elizabeth and this must be fully functional by the end of the month.

Dynamic preference

Dynamic preference

By *low dynamic preference* I mean that some people are better at finishing one task before moving on to the next. Others, who have *high dynamic preference*, are bored and unmotivated without several projects on the go at once. Ignore this at your peril! If you have a number of projects but prefer to complete single tasks before starting a new task, then special efforts will be helpful to ensure success in all projects. The careful structuring of your work and incorporating all projects into one overarching plan may be particularly useful. You may need to structure windows of effort for each job. Psychological tricks, such as clearing every other job physically off the desk, can help too. Likewise, if approaching a colleague who needs to complete a job before starting another, then try to make your approaches in the spaces between their tasks.

Selecting people of high dynamic preference to head up single projects is not a good idea, however successful they may have been in multitask project management previously.

Both extremes of preference have something to offer to Teams. People who are failing in their job may be failing simply because they have too few tasks to maintain their motivation, or too many. In an ideal Team, all the individuals recognise their own preference as well as those of all the others in that Team. This permits an optimum number of projects or reporting lines to be managed by each person. However, in my experience, it is very rare to find this awareness in organisations, with obvious results.

Completer preference

A *completer* focuses on achieving goals. You can appreciate from your knowledge of other preferences that a mix of preferences can manifest in very different ways. A completer could have any of the above preferences, but many successful salespeople are likely to have a mixed preference for in-time and future: an eye on the present and a firm goal fixed in the future. Completers are goal-oriented but their motivations are as varied as human nature. For some it is a competition versus colleagues. For others it is the bank balance next month. For others it is immediate cash in hand or the avoidance of financial ruin. Understanding the motivation and creating an environment that provides the right type of incentive is critical to success.

Goal-setting completers often make excellent but demanding managers. Their focus on goals can mean that they fail to recognise that others need to enjoy the journey towards those goals. Ron came to run a large business via the accountancy route. He was phenomenally bright and well respected but lacked empathy with people and was rather inept socially. The people who worked for him spent many hours sharing stories about him and complaining. A number of them coped less well with the environment that Ron headed and left the business. Awareness and attention to the needs of staff is important if motivation is to be effective in Teams run by this type.

Convincer and decisive preferences

A friend's eight-year-old daughter had been told to go to bed three times and still sat playing in the kitchen. Exasperated, my friend said, 'I've told you three times to go to bed. How many times do I have to tell you!' To which her daughter replied, 'Four times, Mummy.' The *convincer preference* in adults operates in the same way. People with this preference need to be told (or to work over) information several times, often in different ways, before moving on to a decision.

You cannot rush a convincer-preference person and expect them to be motivated. They can be enormously effective when convinced and the key element is *getting* them convinced. Take time to deliver information in different ways and from different sources. Repeat this several times, and involve others.

Someone with a *decisive preference*, on the other hand, is immediately committed. People with this preference can be widely different in their other preferences, since the internal decision-making process may depend, for example, on logical thought or, in contrast, on kinaesthetic feel-good or feel-bad factors (or towards and away-from factors). Because decisive-preference people come to decisions fast, it can be important to encourage them to think through consequences using language that appeals to their other preferences. Some will become easily dispirited or take on other 'exciting projects' and so may start a pattern of failing. If this is not quickly addressed, the pattern may become unproductive and a drain on the resources of the Team.

Match and mismatch preferences

Match and *mismatch* preferences concern the qualities of similarity and difference. Match-preference people look for sameness, whereas mismatch-preference people seek difference. (Populations are broadly split between these two preferences, giving advertisers a real challenge in appealing to both types!) A preference for mismatching is vital in accounting, auditing, statistical process control and quality management. The preference is often so well developed in auditors and other professions needing acute observations of difference, that it sometimes affects many other aspects of their work and social life. Match preference, on the other hand, is useful in customer-service and sales jobs. Within Teams, it is important to explore both these preferences, since persistent matching (although very appealing and friendly) may lead to poor creativity and innovation. While this may not matter in low-technology, low-threat markets, it would be a killer in international IT if people in top Teams all matched one another. We may be frustrated by difference but we need to welcome it as essential to high Team performance.

Because match-preference people are looking for sameness, it is important to motivate them by highlighting this aspect.

For example:

> The merger is a simple extension of our existing business with our products and company name continuing to be sold as before.

For people with a mismatch preference, information about difference needs to be highlighted:

> The merger marks a significant shift from service – to product-based business in the medical field in particular. This will provide

us with a unique position in our market and one that gives us a tremendous lead over the others in our chosen field.

It may be necessary to embrace both preferences to appeal to everyone in a Team:

The merger is a logical extension of our core business. Our company name and brands will predominate but there will be opportunities for the development of novel products that will single us out as innovators in our market.

How do you get a mismatch-preference person to agree with you? Imagine that your research has established that customers prefer blue rather than yellow motorbikes this year and you believe that blue is the way to go. Your manager will decide, but she is a mismatch-preference person. To get her agreement you could make a feature out of the difference in the proposed blue and might say, 'Maybe we should stick to yellow.' With luck she will want to mismatch you!

Internally and externally referenced preferences

Any person may use different thinking processes in different situations. There is a chance, though, that you and others have a preference for either deciding *internally* about something or needing third-party (*external*) information and judgment before action. If you wish your report to appeal to a predominantly externally referenced person, then include supporting statements other than your own. (It may be helpful to work out what your own preference is. How do *you* reach decisions? How important are the views of others? Are you self-sufficient, basing decisions on information only, or do you need to discuss issues with others?)

To elicit your colleague's preference, just ask him how he reached a decision about some action he took at work. If he describes his own thoughts, preferences and actions then he is likely to be internally referenced. If he talks about referring to the views or discussions of others, then he's likely to be externally referenced. Remember that preferences are context-specific, so the question needs to be related to work. Someone who acts spontaneously at work may research in great deal before selecting a car or builder.

All the above preferences can be developed within people through training – but it is well to recognise preference types and their strengths and weaknesses in setting up project Teams.

Culture change

Understanding your own thinking preferences permits you to make planned behavioural differences. These new behaviours can create downstream development within the Team. That is, through repetition of set patterns of behaviour. That means that change is measurable. These patterns in the Team are 'the way we do things' and normally evolve with time. The evolution of the culture is a mixture of natural growth and planned influence.

Some of the patterns are, or become, dysfunctional. The process of understanding the way we think offers us powerful choices for change. Individual choice and action gives each of us the possibility of stimulating local changes, which, if repeated elsewhere in the Team, creates cultural change.

Review

Let's review what we have covered. Thinking preferences include:

- left- and right-brain
- visual
- auditory
- kinaesthetic
- linguistic
- interpersonal
- creative
- systematic/procedural
- numerical
- away-from and towards
- big-picture
- detailed picture

- past, in-time and future
- dynamic
- completer
- convincer and decisive
- match and mismatch
- internal and external
- personal change impacting on culture change.

Chapter Two

Similarity and Difference

Summary

This chapter broadens awareness of the interesting differences between how we think and do things compared with others. Through quick exercises, it also aims to provide a more comprehensive understanding of our own motivation and that of others too.

Similarity and difference help explain why things work or do not work in organisations. Checking our own similarities and differences and comparing these with the Team can be like shining a powerful light into a dark space: suddenly everything is clearer. One model for checking out similarity and difference is that of Gregory Bateson,[3] who describes a concept where there are several levels of thinking and experiencing. In outline, these are:

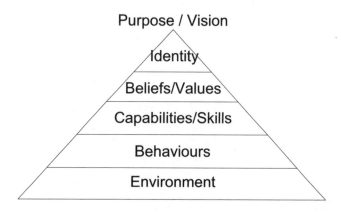

Purpose / Vision

Identity

Beliefs/Values

Capabilities/Skills

Behaviours

Environment

The model is hierarchical. The upper levels influence more than those below. The lower levels dominate more than those above. If our environment is freezing, then our behaviours and skills are dominated by the environment and we are forced to make

---

[3] Adapted after Bateson (1992) by Dilts (1994).

changes. On the other hand, if we establish a purpose (top level) to help others, then this will influence how we behave and what skills we seek to acquire.

The model also suggests to us that we are unlikely to stop smoking by altering behaviour unless a compelling reason exists higher up the diagram. In other words, I need to make a shift in my values about health (for example) or perhaps re-evaluate my sense of identity and self-image as a nonsmoker. Changing the environment by removing the ashtrays is unlikely to make a difference. A changing *value* about health might make this difference because *value* is higher up the list. The model is helpful, since it gives another opportunity to clarify our thinking and to check for match and mismatch with the thinking of people within the Team (or with the Team's profile overall). There is a particular value in going through entire Teams using this approach (see Pritchard, 1997, for instance), but I will leave this challenge largely up to the reader to explore. For the purposes of this book it will be useful to work through the levels for yourself and use the learning that comes from that process to create new opportunities for improvement.

Environment

Our environment for working, once the basic needs for comfort, light and sound quality have been fulfilled, is of different importance for different people. Many corporations ignore the need for personal individuality and preferences for the sake of uniformity and single identity (and often this is where the corporation has some meaningless mission statement valuing the individual!). For many of us, the working environment is important. Comfort, light and background noise levels contribute to both mood and efficiency.

Exercise

If environment is important for you, how does your current working environment rate against your ideal? What, if anything, could you change for improved comfort and efficiency? Look through the list and add other criteria that are significant for your ideal. Then, set down your ratings (ten is high) for your *current* office space.

Environmental quality	Now	I can change
Light:		
brightness		
glare		
evenness		
degree of shadow		
sound level and quality		
cleanliness		
Furniture:		
chair type		
desk height		
colour scheme		
storage: position and type		
folders: colours and indexing system		
Personal effects:		
pictures and photographs		
gifts		
Other:		

Where can you make a change that will make a difference? Make a note of it and set down actions to accomplish it to a specific timescale. Be sure that you are in control of each action. If you need the permission or approval of someone else, then break the action down into smaller steps. Your first action may then become, 'I will speak with Geoffrey on Wednesday morning about disconnecting my fluorescent strips and installing some bulb lighting.'

Behaviours

While behaviours may seem to be low on the influencing scale, they can provide a great source of information for personal change and efficacy. An example of this is my own experience in an international company with headquarters in the US. When writing to colleagues, I found that my memos became shorter and more clipped. Without my realising it, some of these efficient communications were missing the need of others to re-establish in their own mind the comfortable relationships that we enjoyed face to face. With no opening greetings or preamble, I would launch into my appreciation of needs and my proposed course of action. Face-to-face feedback told me that the style was not always appreciated. I therefore made my communications a little more friendly.

This was not as difficult as it might have been, but I was surprised that I felt the additional words clashed with my own value about efficiency. I also realised that somewhere along my career development I had arrived at the belief that, if I could not communicate a letter on one page, then I was somehow lacking in effective communication! To change my writing style without it conflicting, I realised that I needed to re-evaluate my beliefs and values. An important step was to reassess the value I place in relationships and Teams. Once these were in place, I no longer had to make an effort concerning each and every communication: they all became friendlier, except when I was overly tired from travelling. Then I continued to have to watch my written word until the new style of writing became fully integrated.

Later, we shall be examining behaviours and values together, to look for the similarities and differences we have compared with our Team or organisation (or one we hope to join). This will provide confirmation about what is OK and will give understanding about where the similarities are poor. Actions can arise from this knowledge in order to make a difference.

Competencies and skills

You may find it useful to note down your current thinking about your personal skills and development needs, if any, that you feel necessary to improve your development both as an individual and as part of a community or Team.

Exercise

For a snapshot of your current thinking, what competencies and skills do you have and what others do you need now or within the foreseeable future? It may also be useful to use the 0–10 rating system to rank these. It can be useful to imagine that you have just become a friendly observer of yourself. To do this, take a step out of yourself and move to a different position (the so-called *observer* or *third* position). Look back to where you were, or imagine yourself in your work environment. What competencies and skills does that person really have? Here is an example:

Competence/skill examples:	Have	Need	How to get that?
telephone selling	6	9	*training course*
filing	4	9	*ask Susan in accounts*
driving	0	10	*book lessons*
time management			
relating with superiors			
relating with peers			
meeting targets			
reporting skills			

Note down any possible actions and check the criteria for successful commitments. Here they are:

Criteria for successful commitments

✓   Is each commitment within my complete control?
✓   Can I give a clear time when I will start?
✓   Can I clearly imagine myself doing this?
✓   Can I imagine a positive result from completing this action?
✓   Can I set a personal and realistic test so that I know when I have satisfied my criteria for success?
✓   What certainty (0–10) do I have that I will achieve each of my commitments?

If you rate lower than 8 on that last score, then you may need to establish a more compelling reason or just remove the commitment from the list.[4]

Prioritisation

What if you have two or more actions with scores of 8 or more? Which one should you do first? Often, having used a logical process to establish the ranking of actions, it is useful to rely on a gut feeling (instinct) to finalise the decision. If our gut feelings run in conflict with our logical decisions then we are likely to struggle, be less effective or fail.

In revaluing my own actions and aims, I often use scoring systems to produce a priority list. Having made the list, I then go through it as if someone else had produced it and say, 'There, this is what you need, a priority list of actions that is absolutely right for you!' I then rely on my feelings about the list. Sometimes these are surprising. And I invariably go with the gut feeling rather than the

---

[4] Some people do consider that 8 is the highest ranking they would ever give, even if permitted to go as far as 10. In cases such as these, it is the significance of the difference between the ranking given and the highest ranking they feel possible that is important.

logical listing. The reason for doing that is that we are motivated and demotivated very much by feelings – if I ignore them, then I can expect trouble later!

Appendix 5 provides another prioritisation process, or ranking process, that cleverly invokes emotional input (albeit surreptitiously) to create priority lists from logical information. It may be time to think about a break in your reading if you have not already done so. Learning is often best accomplished with gaps for other activities or rest every fifteen to twenty minutes. It also helps to have regular reviews of work in summary.

If our gut-feelings run in conflict with our logical decisions then we are likely to struggle, be less effective or fail.

Values

If you have recently worked on values and are clear about them, then skip this section. If you have not, or if you have experienced personal development since your last value elicitation, then it may be useful to stay with the process and explore again.

For the avoidance of any doubt, let me say now that, by values, I mean: *those fundamental qualities that you hold most precious.*

The benefit of knowing these values is that they provide us with a powerful set of criteria against which we can match all other personal decisions and actions. Values are very influencing. Often this influence isn't 'noticed' by the individual because most of us do not make decisions by referring to them. Instead, our values permeate our decisions and behaviours. We are happier when we operate to support our values rather than to undermine them. Bringing values regularly into our conscious decision making makes the process easier and our resulting actions more committed. It becomes so much easier to make decisions if they can be based on personal values.

Our values permeate our decisions and behaviours.

An example of this is an experience of my own. An employee was drafted into our offices some years back. Unfortunately, he had some problems with his personal hygiene and the smell was nauseating. Colleagues would open windows during the winter season, even though the building was air-conditioned, but no one seemed able to approach him. I felt compelled to do something and tried to work out the best approach. I knew that we would soon be receiving a royal visitor and my value about the standards exhibited in my organisation could not be met with this new colleague in the building. On the other hand, I did not feel it appropriate to speak to him myself. Neither my colleagues nor I had developed any kind of friendship with him and this made it more difficult. In the absence of an obvious friend, I spoke with his boss in private. He already knew of the problem but had not faced it either. I explained my concerns and soon noticed a change.

Exercise

Here are some examples, and a chart in which you may set down your own rating for the importance of each value in the column 'Value rating':

Value	Value rating (0–10)	My actions rating
Example: I value honesty	10	10
Example: I value compassion	6	4
Example: I value success (in meeting budgets)	7	8
Example: I value clarity of thinking	6	5
Example: I value quality of communication	4	6
I value		
I value		
I value		
I value		
I value		

How well do you exemplify your values in your actions at work? In the next column, labelled 'My actions rating', set down your rating for the level at which, on average, you feel that you exhibit these values by your actions and deeds. This rating will represent your actual manifestation of that value in what you *do*. It may be necessary to set down a band of ratings (e.g. 2–6 or 3–9) for differing circumstances. When you have completed this, look for difference in the two sets of values. Most often, we find a mismatch between some of the ratings and/or flexibility in how we demonstrate those values in practice!

Where this is the case, it can be motivating to establish actions for changing behaviours. Ask these questions, for example:

- Where, when and with whom did I not meet my own value rating?
- What could I have done differently to rectify that?
- Would that make a positive difference for me?
- Would this new strategy work next time around? When? With whom?
- Can I make a commitment to that?

Dominic values quality relationships at work. He says that, for him, quality is openness, ease of communication and especially humour. Dominic works in drug safety and realised that his communication with Lola, the divisional health and safety officer, was not good. He found that his ability to communicate effectively with Lola did not meet his own value score at any of his recent meetings with her. He thought about a recent time and wondered what he might have done to improve the situation and what would have made a positive difference for him.

He realised that he was defensive and cold and that his *anticipation* of acrimony could be making things worse. He thought about how he could have been more physically relaxed and maybe more warm towards Lola. Perhaps he could have made a joke of something. He then thought about the next meeting he would have and how he could prepare himself to operate differently with her. He was certain he could achieve a better level of relaxation and warmth. He committed himself to doing just that. Since that time, their relationship has gone from strength to strength.

Sensory journeys

We note that Dominic projected ahead to experience future scenarios in those meetings with Lola. To begin with, there is logical thinking about the scenarios, when they might meet, where, what they may say. Another valuable step is to go on a *sensory journey* (sometimes referred to as *future pacing*). In this case, Dominic would mentally allow the clock to spin forward and imagine that the meeting was taking place now. The chances are that he would be able to see the situation and hear the spoken words as if they were actually happening in real time. The advantage of that is that Dominic learns more about the scenario and especially his emotional reactions to it. Since emotion is a powerful motivator (and demotivator), this process is critical in assessing his commitment to action.

When you have worked through any examples of your own using the above questions, check out any commitments using your confidence score and work through the criteria for successful commitments used earlier. Before leaving this section, please note where your scores are matched. It is worth acknowledging these before moving on to look at beliefs and identity.

Beliefs

Beliefs, as I illustrated in the tale about overcoming my writing style, can be empowering. Changing my belief that 'short equals efficient' and making my memos friendlier made a significant difference. Beliefs can be limiting as well as empowering. Limiting beliefs leave us power-*less*, like victims of circumstance and time. Each time we give away the control of what happens, we become less powerful, and a spiral of underachieving may start.

Limiting beliefs

Limiting beliefs

Listed below are just a few examples of limiting beliefs. Many others can be heard on trains and buses, in shops and restaurants the world over.

- Women are poor managers.
- You can never trust a ... (insert nationality/affiliation or religion).
- Corporate strategies never get anybody anywhere.
- There is no such thing as Team spirit, everybody is competitive.
- When you get to age forty, you're going nowhere.
- No one will ever notice if I work more efficiently.
- If the company don't give you the car you want, they don't want you.
- People always harbour a grudge, whatever they say.
- When it happens, it happens. I mean, what can you do?

The words *always* and *never* often crop up in limiting beliefs, e.g. Taxis *never* come when you want one; you wait for an hour and then the buses always come in threes!

**Limiting beliefs leave us powerless, like victims
of circumstance and time.**

To be a performance manager it is important to be able to review
our beliefs and prejudices. This is not always hard to do and what
makes it easier is practice. Let's look first at the opposite of limiting beliefs: *empowering beliefs*.

Empowering beliefs

Empowering beliefs

I remember having a major crisis over the writing of a complex corporate bid. I could not get started on the project. The difference
was made when I reviewed some of the other difficult writing
assignments I had successfully completed in spite of my earlier
reservations. I acknowledged that the assignments had sometimes
been difficult but that I had achieved something useful afterwards.
This challenge looked bigger. How could I possibly get my thinking around it?

My empowering beliefs were these:

- I believe that I can complete this difficult project as I have done
  before.

- I believe that, by breaking the project down into smaller sections of effort, I can make progress and gain confidence.

Empowering beliefs give you back control. They engender confidence and power. They are part of the ammunition of successful managers.

Here are some examples that prove useful:

- My identity is growing and changing all the time.
- Flexibility in thinking makes a major difference to performance.
- I can work with anybody.
- I have, or have access to, all the resources I need to do this task.
- I alone am responsible for my progress.
- I do have choices.
- Changing or taking on a belief does not change my identity or me.

This last belief is critically important if we are to get to new levels of learning and effectiveness. Many people feel uncomfortable when starting personal change. Their patch of safety is somehow threatened. But life has a habit of catching up with managers who are limited in mental flexibility. With hindsight, it is better and more empowering to stimulate one's own flexibility than have it forced due to painful circumstances.

Try one or more of the beliefs above for yourself – or another of your own construction. If it helps, step into a *new you*, by moving just one pace into a *new you having that belief*. Really notice what difference the belief makes. When you have fully embraced that new belief, think about situations in which that new belief would have made a difference – or could do so in the future:

- How would I have behaved differently?
- What difference might that have made to what happened?
- What would it be like next time?
- What would I do or say next time?
- What level of confidence do I have about that?

You might also consider a sensory journey to explore a possible future scenario, holding the new belief as if it were happening now.

It is better and more empowering to stimulate one's own flexibility than have it forced due to painful circumstances.

An example of where empowering beliefs can make a difference
Jenny got into an argument with Sarah that was not resolved. It concerned some work that Jenny did. Sarah's recall was that she, Sarah, was going to do it. But later she found out that Jenny had done the work. Jenny did remember *discussing it*. Jenny also felt that she would do it better and faster than Sarah could. Jenny feels that Sarah is often snotty with her and that she is probably envious of Jenny's superior position.

Suggested empowering beliefs for Jenny
- Sarah feels intimidated by me.
- Sarah feels vulnerable generally.
- I can stay calm when challenged.
- I am secure in my role.
- Sarah would be much happier if I encouraged her more.

Suggested empowering beliefs for Sarah
- Jenny is often forgetful about detail with everybody.
- I could help by summarising agreements in writing.
- If I communicated what was important to me, it would help us both.
- Our combined output is higher when we work together.

Empowering beliefs provide new perceptions, new horizons and the possibility of new levels of performance. In every interaction that is less than perfect, there is the possibility of learning through the use of empowering beliefs. In this way I function better as a manager and my Team functions better, too.

It does not matter if the belief is true, since the result of 'taking on' the new belief is to change one's perception of the situation. This leads to a change in one's behaviour, including, subconsciously, one's language and tone. Although this does not guarantee success in a subsequent interaction with the same person, it is likely to make a positive difference. That is one more choice than doing the same thing badly again and repeating the cycle of poor interaction. It may be *their* problem or fault, but only *you* can make a difference if your counterpart does not choose to.

Identity

I am not my values.
I am not my beliefs.
I am not my feelings.
I am not my purpose.
I am not what I do.
So, what am I?

If I am not what I do, then what am I? Am I a thinking brain within a body, or a body with thoughts? Is the 'I' part separate from the mortal, physical me? In other words, am I the thoughts and ideas *independent* of my brain and body? I could think of myself as a trainer or coach but I am different from other trainers and coaches, so are those descriptions enough to satisfy my own need for identity? They really describe *what I do* rather than *who I am*. You can establish your own sense of identity by philosophical ideas or by identifying characteristics and descriptions of what you do. The important thing is self-knowledge and comfort with those descriptions. Some people have a strong sense of their own identity without the need for actual words to express what they inherently know. Sometimes one just knows!

Practically everyone you know has been changing his or her identity consciously or unconsciously. The people who do not change as time goes on are anachronistic and very easy to spot. Somehow, time leaves them behind and their behaviours become more and more bizarre – unless of course fashion catches up with them! Platform shoes looked rather silly in the early nineties but by 1998 were back in vogue. In 2006, they again look ridiculous. Surely, then, our identities must be changing, or we too would become out of pace with the world around us.

Acknowledging or 'taking on' the belief that our identity is a grow-ing, changing thing is powerful. Very often the fear of identity change stops us from taking risks and doing new things because 'it's just not me', even when sometimes we do want to do some-thing different. Thus, fear of change in self can restrain us from reaching our goals and leading fulfilled lives. Fully taking on board the empowering belief that growth and change in identity is OK provides the subconscious with permission actually to allow change to happen. Taking on beliefs is one of the most significant strategies for personal development available to us (another key skill is using feedback for self-awareness and learning). This process substantially shifts managing ability to new levels of performance.

Fear of change in self can restrain us from reaching our goals.

I had a girlfriend once whose sense of identity was very fragile. She continuously looked for new careers. She was really looking to fit into an identity that she thought the new career would give her. Similarly, being in a relationship for her meant developing a role that could provide her with a sense of who she was. She was more or less unhappy before, during and after we finished our relation-ship. It did not help that her sense of self-worth was low, even though she had so many good attributes. Her searching went on.

Identity is not just about what job we have and the clothes we wear. It includes a unique set of manifestations, values and beliefs as well. These can help define an idea of identity. A good sense of purpose in life also helps. When you know what you are here for, the lower levels, including identity, can all fit into place.

Purpose and vision

What is the highest level of purpose that you have for what you do in your life?

Examples might include:

1.   to make money
2.   to get promotion to VP

3. to provide for my family
4. to be creative
5. to exemplify what is best in all I do as defined by my religion.

In order to seek clarity of vision for ourselves, it is useful to be specific. Expanding on the examples above may help to illustrate this:

1. to make enough money to pay off the loans on my property by 31 December in three years' time
2. to achieve VP status by July next year or move company
3. to increase reserves to two times my net salary (by end of the tax year in five years' time)
4. to publish two technical papers by the end of next year
5. to read the scriptures for two hours each week on Friday evenings.

Each example has transformed into a *specific goal* and a *time frame* for achieving that goal.

Now, many people feel that their purpose is not significant enough. If you find this also, then try to explore your feelings about the following:

I want ...

- to do the best that I am able
- to grow and develop as much as I can
- to put back more than I take out
- to achieve a balance between work, family and personal indulgence that I feel comfortable with
- to retire with a good pension
- to work and provide for my family and to write two books
- to love and sustain my family and friends and support and encourage my colleagues
- to survive each day and each week.

Exercise: Purpose and vision

No.	Purpose/vision
1	
2	
3	
4	

Whatever your own sense of purpose, it is potentially the greatest motivator you can have in your life. Einstein's incredible life work was not about mathematics or physics but about exploring his understanding about God. The higher you can elevate your sense of purpose, the greater potential you give yourself for achieving more with each second. And decision making becomes easier once we understand what our purpose is, who we are as individuals, what our values are and what our beliefs are. Purpose provides the ultimate context for making all decisions. These decisions become faster and easier with experience. Purpose unleashes performance.

In order of influence: the levels are purpose, identity, values and beliefs, capabilities and skills, behaviour and environment. If one value is about helping others it may be more or less easy to find the context for that at work, say, as a mortuary manager. In an ideal world our work and life references would be identical and it is certainly useful to see how, at each level, our purpose, identity etc. fit with our work.

It is also useful to look at each level *specifically* in the context of work. 'What is my purpose at work?' 'What do I value at work?' Where these support our personal life there is an enhancement in influence – but sometimes you may find areas where there is apparent conflict. These give scope for personal change and development.

An example of time when I had a clash of values was to do with how I did (and did not) care about other people. Years ago I cared for people in my private and business worlds, but there were those who did not meet my expectation or who did not share my vision. I could be quite callous with those people. Big men sometimes cried in my office. The greater influence of my sense of purpose *in the context of work* (success at any cost) led to a conflict in values and resulting differences in behaviours inside and outside work. It was only when I raised my value (for taking care of people) to being a part of my overarching purpose *in any context* (and now including at work) that my behaviours at work changed for the better – for me and the people working around me!

Compulsion: Heading towards goals

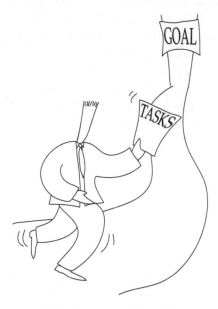

Heading towards goals

In going through the process of self-exploration, you have probably made some decisions about actions that need to be taken. If you have done this and checked your ranking under 'Criteria for successful commitments' above, then you are already some way towards achieving your goals – assuming of course that your sense of identity allows for such success! Additional compulsion or motivation can come from having an experience of achieving goals now, in the present. I call these *sensory journeys* as described earlier but below I add another dimension to them. The word *vision* evokes the need to picture *visually* that purpose or goal, but there are other components of that experience also. When I started out writing the first edition of this book, the idea of spending weeks writing, rewriting and taking criticism was not a stimulating one. If my thinking had stopped there, no book would have been written – but looking towards, and *experiencing* the future, seeing and feeling the cover of the complete book, signing off copies and receiving letters from around the world became a more compelling experience rather than just an idea. After my sensory journey it was a simpler task to break the goal into smaller goals and commence work.

We have many resistances to getting sales, finishing reports, speaking to a colleague about our concerns and other things. Creating a compelling future and experiencing it in the present is a powerful way of motivating and of increasing our learning of how to get there more simply and more quickly.

Timelines – sensory journeys with movement

Walk the timeline

One novel way to experience the future is to walk – physically – *imaginary* journeys to our goals. These journeys are called *timelines* (see, for example, Hall and Bodenhamer, 1997). This whole journey can be done in your head, but you may find it helpful actually to walk the timeline during the process. The advantage of this is that you experience biofeedback from your body in relation to movement and direction. This can be very helpful in fully experiencing the journey and gaining the greatest possible motivation and learning from it. Thus, physical movement can add to the sensory journey so it becomes more 'real'. The object is to experience fully each time frame on the timeline *as if* it were happening in the present moment. To do that, you have to let your virtual clock run forward a leap at each step. Timeline work demands versatility and an inquisitive, open mind. Before starting on the timeline, decide where it starts, and have in mind an exact place where you can walk to that defines the objective in both space and in time.

The timeline starts with now.[5] Before doing anything else, it is important to centre yourself fully (ideally while standing) by noticing as much as you can about your current state and your surroundings. Typical questions to ask yourself are:

- How do I feel throughout my body?
- Where, if anywhere, am I tense?
- What quality does the light have?
- Are there any noises?
- Am I aware of my pulse or breathing?

The next step is to note your imaginary timeline extending into the future to the place that you have already identified. That place will also have a specific date in the future associated with it. Having imagined that point on the line where you will have achieved your specific goal, begin walking the line, stopping to notice key people and interactions, key choices and decisions that must be made on the journey. At each stopping point, check out fully your experience, both internally and externally. Move on only when you have an experience of *actually being there*, which is 8 or more out of 10, where 10 would be your concept of perfection.

At your goal, fully notice what the experience is like.

- What is happening around me?
- Who is here?
- What are they saying?
- What else can I hear, feel and see?
- Is my breathing or my body feeling any different?
- Do I need anything else to make this goal a reality, and, if so, what is that missing piece?

---

[5] If you have a friend or colleague who would like to coach you through the process, that would be an advantage. They do not need to be a trained coach. Get them to go through the process using present-tense language (if they speak at any point on the line). For example, 'So, you say it's March 2012 and you are on the corporate board – what are you experiencing now?'

- Is this goal significant and compelling enough for me to really *have to* achieve it?

The experience is completed by returning along the timeline to *now*. This can provide more learning and information. Pause at *each point* of choice/experience as before.

- What (if anything) am I experiencing differently?
- Does this choice or experience seem easier than before, and, if it does, how is it different?

When you get back to where you started, turn and look at the point where you experienced your goal. Ask yourself:

- Can I make the journey shorter or quicker?
- Does the goal seem easier or more difficult to reach than before?

If it is done successfully, you should have a higher confidence score after walking your timeline than you did before. In addition, the actual steps where other choices, experiences and decision making are needed should be clearer. Your real-life experience of the journey should also be easier. You know exactly where you are going and what it takes to get there.

Review

Let's review what we have covered:

- We explored the six levels of thinking and experience.
- In order of their influence and in reverse order of dominance these are: purpose and vision; values/beliefs; identity; capabilities/skills; behaviours; and environment.
- We used the criteria for successful commitments to check our intended actions.
- We established a definitive priority list of actions.
- We identified both limiting and empowering beliefs and tried some on.
- We introduced the idea of experiencing sensory journeys in order to gain a greater sense of our motivation.

- We used a timeline to get an experience of what a future goal is like, and to learn from that in the present.

A note on external Teams

This book does not go into an in-depth exploration of similarity and difference using the model described in this chapter.[6] Suffice, then, to write that the model is a useful tool for comparing self with the characteristics of the Team as a whole and for looking at interpersonal similarity and difference. Performed in the context of some good empowering beliefs and a broad and embracing value base, the techniques allow for the Team to grow and operate at entirely new levels of performance and trust. The management of the information is more important than the method used for obtaining it!

---

[6] But please see Chapter 3, which introduces a new model for that.

Chapter Three

Me and My Team:
Same or Different?

Break the goals into smaller goals (see page 39)

Summary

In this chapter, we will review the level of similarity and difference between your personal values (and characteristics) and those of the Team. These are quick methods of gaining information about what is functional and dysfunctional in Teams, providing new choices of personal action for success. Let's get some insights and learning by characterising behaviours.

Exercise: Corporate characteristics

These exercises are designed to raise awareness of you in relation to your organisation, but are also useful to gain greater understanding of what you do not want and what you do want in your new job and Team. Imagine, if you will, that you are regarding the Team as a single person with a name, e.g. John Ace-Computer, Celia Engineering, April Training, Paul IT.

This person has a number of characteristics, and I would like you to rate your perception of what those are on the list on the next page. ratings are from 0–10 (where 10 is high). Please leave the other columns blank for now.

It may be helpful to look down the ratings and double-check them. Do you like this person? Have you discovered anything new about them? Look for difference and indicate where you could have some serious difficulty in relating with them.

When you have completed all the ratings, let's find out whether this person acts in a way that is aligned with their values or whether they have values which they ignore in their actions. An example might be a company that has very strictly managed timekeeping methods but has senior managers who ignore this in their own behaviours. This provides useful information in deciding how we might behave in order to improve relationships in the Team. In the 'Value' column, rate what *that person/organisation* values about those characteristics. A good trick is to imagine that you are this Team person, stepping into this person's life and taking on all their characteristics and ratings. Do that now and note down the values from the perspective of that person.

There is often important learning in the 'Value' column, and to find it we need to look for difference between what the *values* are and what the *ratings* are. Where these are widely different, your Team has a major problem. This is worth recognising, since your own behaviours can never match those of the Team!

Team name _____

Characteristic	Rate	Value	My rate	My value
Example only: short (0) – neutral (5) – tall (10)	7			
male (0) female (10)				
childish (0) adult/mature (10)				
manipulative & controlling (0) easygoing (10)				
poorly organised (0) excellently organised (10)				
lacks values (0) has clear values (10)				
lacks identity (0) striking identity (10)				
no vision (0) clear vision (10)				
fearful of change (0) embraces change (10)				
poor learning skills (0) inquisitive learner (10)				
inflexible (0) flexible (10)				
unimaginative (0) creative/innovative (10)				
solo player (0) full Team player (10)				
lazy (0) hard-working(10)				
lacks motivation (0) motivated (10)				
passive (0) aggressive (10)				
deaf (0) superb listener (10)				
dislikes challenge (0) open to feedback (10)				
quiet (0) loud (10)				
poor communicator (0) good communicator (10)				
poor technical skills (0) good technical skills (10)				
poor management skills (0) good manager (10)				
poor time manager (0) excellent time manager (10)				
misses targets (0) meets or exceeds targets (10)				
poor in relationships (0) good in relationships (10)				
conceited (0) affable (10)				
dishonest (0) honest (10)				
secretive (0) open (10)				
discouraging (0) encouraging (10)				
dishonest (0) trustworthy (10)				
ego-free (0) ego big and sensitive (10)				
OTHERS:				

Characteristic	Rate	Value	My rate	My value
Example only: unimaginative (0) – creative/innovative (10)	7	3		

Management may have a clear new culture policy about valuing innovation, which it says it wishes to encourage and cascade through the organisation. But in reality the policy may be lip service to management posturing. In effect, those employees who demonstrate innovation may be punished for having done so. In this type of organisation you are in a no-win situation. If you do not innovate then you do not fit the declared wants of the organisation. If you do innovate then you do not fit what the organisation really wants. In effect, this causes the politically aware employee to talk about innovation but not actually do it, thereby encouraging the lie throughout the organisation and debilitating it. I was once in a meeting and told that the company was encouraging responsibility and risk taking even if mistakes were made. They also said that the CEO was behind the policy, but still cited individual mistakes made five years ago! There are countless examples of these dishonest behaviours in many companies, including the big bluechips, government and public services.

What other choices are there? Discussing the mismatch with management is hardly likely to be welcome unless the organisation rates very highly on the open-to-feedback characteristic (see table). Alternatively, you can take the dishonest, theatrical approach illustrated above and talk *as if* you matched that characteristic (which the Team says it wants) but make sure that you do not actually exemplify that in your actions! You can take a middle rating and play safe. You can find a new Team if the conflict is one that makes you feel very uncomfortable.

The next part of the test is to use the 'My rate' column to set down your own characteristics. But before you do this I will ask you again to alter your perspective. The best way to do this may be physically to leave the place where you are standing or sitting and, in doing so, 'leave yourself' behind. In effect, step out of yourself and become a detached 'observer'. An actual physical move helps. Take a look at yourself from outside and fill in the ratings under 'My rate' for how you manifest each characteristic.

Characteristic	Rate	Value	My rate	My value
Example only: unimaginative (0) – creative/innovative (10)	7	3	**6**	

Now that you have done the 'My rate', entries, take a look at similarities and differences compared with the 'Rate' column for the Team. In what way do your characteristics fit or not fit those of your Team?

Below, note down where the fit or similar criterion is poorest between 'My rate' and 'Rate' (for the Team).

Difference of exemplified characteristics between me and my Team:

Now, for each of those you have written down, note whether your rating errs towards the value level of the Team or the other way? Please note down where these similarities and differences lie, and, in particular, where your own rating varies markedly from either the 'My rate' or 'Value' level of the Team.

Worst scenario of difference between my characteristics and my Team's characteristics and values:

You may have already decided that there are changes that you can make in order to operate better in the Team. But before you move ahead to action planning, let's complete the cycle of checking with the final step. This is to place your rating for each characteristic in the 'My value' column.

Characteristic	Rate	Value	My rate	My value
Example only: unimaginative (0) – creative/innovative (10)	7	3	6	8

In particular, note any difference between your demonstrated characteristics ('My rate') and the values you actually place in those characteristics ('My value'). It is very common for the two ratings to vary in some areas. Where they do, it may be relatively easy to make commitments to changing your behaviours in order to match more closely your value ratings (for those characteristics). I would urge you to write down your commitments (if any) in the box below. In making any commitments, note especially where these will bring you closer to those exemplified by the Team rating. And, if it does not, then maybe ask yourself whether the change will be valued by the Team or not. This process offers you a whole new set of choices about your behaviours and how you can manifest them in the Team – both for your own personal satisfaction and that of the Team.

Look at the boxes above. Is there any characteristic that remains without an action that would bring you closer to the characteristics of the Team or the values that the Team gives to these characteristics? If there is, then you may wish to commit to action.

Commitments for changing my behaviours:

Let's just check that the commitments pass the test for success.

Criteria for successful commitments: new behaviours

✓ Is each commitment within my complete control?
✓ Can I give a clear time when I will start?
✓ Can I clearly imagine myself doing this?
✓ Can I remember a specific and recent time when I could have behaved differently?
✓ Can I imagine a positive result if I had behaved differently?
✓ Can I set a personal and realistic test so that I know when I have satisfied my criteria for successfully implementing this change?
✓ What certainty (0–10) do I have that I will achieve each of my commitments?

If you rate less than 8 on that last rating, then you may need to establish a more compelling reason to change. Or just remove the commitment from the list. I urge this because your Team needs you to be successful. If you fail to follow your own commitments then you will sometimes manifest failure in the Team also.

Observer learning

In looking at the difference between the corporate and your own characteristics, you were asked to imagine being an observer of self. This method is similar to the sensory journey and timeline in that you are experiencing things as if they were real. In the example, you were asked to imagine leaving your body in order to observe yourself objectively and remotely (left behind). This is to detach from any emotional factors and seek clinical and objective information that might not otherwise have been accessible. Observer learning can also be obtained by the same technique in relation to other people. You might detach from a situation in order to seek new clarity about what may be driving their behaviours.

Review

Let's review what we have covered:

- We looked for internal and external Team match and mismatch.
- We tested this by looking at the Team as if it were an individual with particular characteristics.
- We set down ratings for the characteristics based on what the Team does, not what it says it does.
- We set down the ratings for how the Team *values* each characteristic and looked for match/mismatch.
- We saw that mismatch causes dilemmas in the Team because the situation is *no-win*.
- We set down ratings for how we manifest the characteristics ourselves in what we do.
- We identified matching and mismatching behaviours between our Team and self.
- We especially noted where our rating differed from both the Team rating and Team value.
- We set down ratings for the way in which we personally value the characteristics.
- We looked for match/mismatch with our personal manifestation of these characteristics and made commitments.
- We checked our criteria for successful commitments, and, if they did not meet these criteria, removed them from the list.
- We explored the use of observer learning to gain objectivity, especially where our self or an uncomfortable situation with another person is being experienced.

A note on external Teams

The technique of looking at a Team or organisation as an individual is one I often use as a starting point with senior management when they are considering a culture-change strategy. It identifies what the company is like and what it aspires to be. I have also used the technique in coaching senior management during merger, to identify HR issues and initiate strategies for testing and then ameliorating any potential issues.

It is useful to do match/mismatch work with entire Teams. In addition to the characteristics chart, it is also useful to do these checks using the Bateson model and include the matching of goals both for the Team and for each person. Where the real benefit comes to the Team is through the management of the feedback (and learning from the process) rather from the actual chosen method itself. Enormous sums of money are spent, for example, on personality tests. Such methods are of no real benefit unless the same degree of thinking and ability is directed at the process of handling that information and of establishing conditions for change as well as genuine commitments and motivation for change.[7] This is particularly where my work, and that of a small number of agencies and consultancies, makes its mark effectively. The watchword for me is *investment*. At the end of the process, how much investment does the employee have in the commitments to change? The breadth of thinking, openness and flexibility that is needed to achieve this level of motivation is something that I hope this book stimulates in managers at all levels.

---

[7] It is also worth mentioning that personality profiling is often used in hiring people or creating personal development plans. In many cases, the tools used measure preferences and do not therefore have any useful measurement of competences. This does not discount the benefits that discussion and coaching have using these tools as an arena for creative exploration and learning.

Chapter Four

Performance Mindsets

Summary

Performance mindsets are thinking strategies for individual and Team performance. These strategies offer choices for improved performance rather than automatic behaviour patterns that may repeat the errors of the past.

In Chapter Two, we spent some time looking at *empowering beliefs*. We also explored how taking these on *as if* they were true makes a major difference to what happens when we interact with other people in the Team. Empowering beliefs help create a positive mindset and allow us to achieve even greater perception. I am going to present these individual empowering beliefs in two parts. The aim of the first part is to construct your individual set of empowering beliefs that are enabling for you. And the aim of the second part is to explore an additional set of beliefs which will make a difference with your Team specifically. Generally, these differentiate easily into two lists, but it is OK if one empowering belief is common to both lists.

Exercise: Beliefs for personal empowerment

I have listed a set of typical beliefs that may be useful. Please strike out or rewrite any that are not right for you. In addition, I have left space for you to add many of your own. Please state these with *positive* words. An example of a *negatively* expressed belief is:

Being shy does not make me weak.

A better (*positive*) way to express this is to write:

Shy people succeed if they choose to, and I can too.

Here are a few suggestions to start you off:

- My resources include both sources of information and people.
- I can accomplish every aspect of my job now (or will do with further training/coaching).
- To ask for help shows strength of character.
- I am in control of my actions and interactions.
- To follow or not to follow is in my field of choice and control.
- I make a useful contribution to my Team.
- To risk is to be brave.
- Mistakes are an opportunity for learning.
- I am largely responsible for whether I get promoted or not.
- Empowering beliefs give new perception and new choices for successful action.
- Most things go smoothly and well.

Go ahead and create some more of your own:

_____

_____

_____

_____

_____

Exercise: Beliefs for team empowerment

I have listed below a set of typical beliefs that may be useful, but please amend them as you wish, and add any others that you think are helpful.

- Both my Team and I are more successful when we all contribute.
- Team performance is much greater than the sum of the individual performances.
- The contribution of 'following' is at least equal to that of leading or facilitating.
- When I follow rather than lead it is my choice to do so.
- Effective communication is the responsibility of the communicator.
- Asking questions achieves understanding and is good.
- Everyone in the Team is better at something than all the others.
- Individual superiority is an affectation, not a reality.

Additional beliefs:

_____

_____

_____

_____

_____

We have already explored the taking on of empowering beliefs and the benefit that comes from new mindsets (however temporary we choose to make them), creating new perspectives, new understanding and improved action. There is another thread to this, which is called *reframing*.

Reframing

To *reframe* an idea, communication or situation means to look openly for other possible meaning or perspectives. The benefit of reframing is in allowing new insights and the possibility of more effective action. Let's look at some examples.

1. My boss has asked me to do something I am uneasy about.

During a meeting, my boss says, 'By the way, I want you to go through that sales plan for the main board again and see if you can shorten it some.' Later, I feel unease. He does not value my work as it is. He has criticised me in front of other colleagues.

The first element of reframing is questioning for greater understanding. This technique is widely employed in transactional analysis (see, for example, Harris, 1973) because the questioning stems from what is called the *adult aspect* of the psyche which encourages rational thinking. Here are some examples:

- What else could be going on here?
- What other possible interpretations could I make?

- What other motivations (not concerning me) could the boss have for wanting the plan shortened?

Answering these questions logically provides other (positive) possibilities, such as:

- My boss may be thinking to have me present the plan to the main board rather than present it himself – hence the need for something concise. He may not wish to tell me his intention in case he changes his mind about the idea.
- My boss wishes to incorporate the plan into the Corporate Business Plan and needs a clear and concise format for that reason.

And one question may lead to another:

- What is my boss's preference for reporting style? Should I generally be more concise and would he welcome this? Why don't I ask him specifically what style he would like the plan written in?

2. My boss has been promoted and I have a new manager.

I feel uneasy. Maybe I should contact my lawyer, since this is not going to work. My new boss comes from a service background and she has no understanding of marketing or its value. One or two comments she is said to have made seem to support the view that marketing should be led by sales management and not the other way around. What can my old boss have been thinking of when he promoted her!

Questioning for greater understanding, I might ask:

- What else could be going on here?
- What other possible interpretations could I make?
- Are there possible strengths in working with her experience that could help me?
- Isn't it normal to feel threatened in this situation?
- Time will provide me with better information and answers.
- What actions can I take to speed this process up?
- Haven't I tried to run away from an uncomfortable situation before?

- If this is a pattern, could I actively change it and look for positive focus in the new situation?

Exercise: Reframing

If you will, think of a situation that has been uncomfortable or difficult for you. Using the reframing methodology, I invite you to answer some of the questions above (or variants of them, in your own words) and see what other perceptions you can find now that may make a difference. The result may be a healthier mindset with which to approach the new boss (for example) – not full of uncertainty and resentment, but feeling constructive and in a mood of optimism, which the new manager may find easier and more compelling to work *with* rather than *against*.

_____

_____

_____

_____

_____

Now let's look at another type of question, one that teases out a different perspective by asking what *higher* or *hidden* purpose or gift there may be in a new situation.

The form of question is this:

> **If there were a higher purpose in my old boss putting this woman in a post above me, what would the learning or gift be for me?**

This leads to a new perception:

Here is an opportunity. My old boss is testing me. I need to put more of my efforts into marketing myself more effectively within the Team. My boss and others will then have a clearer idea of my contribution and commitment. Maybe I have taken it for granted that, because I do my job well, everyone should know how good I am. Improved communication skills would help. I can get those.

My old boss was always urging me to take more time out for training courses. Maybe now is the time to do that. This new woman has service skills that could offer new thinking about the way I run my division. Putting some ideas to her and involving her actively in that process of new thinking might establish a very good working relationship and encourage her to support me herself!

This higher-purpose idea is a fanciful notion, a simple mental trick, but it often works to one's advantage. I hope you see the potential for finding motivation from a situation by reframing it rather than getting stuck in a patch of acute discomfort which does no good.

Exercise: Higher purpose

Taking your own issue, or another difficult experience you have had, use the question of higher purpose to see what new perspectives you can find. What difference does that make to your understanding? What would have helped you then? If you go on a sensory journey to experience the next potential situation, will this new understanding help you?

_____

_____

_____

_____

_____

Review

Let's review what we have covered:

- We explored the use of beliefs for empowerment, for both the individual and the Team.
- We looked at the use of reframing and two key elements of the reframing process.
- Asking questions that increase understanding.
- Asking questions that look for the higher purpose or gift in a situation.

A note on external Teams

The individual use of questioning, reframing and empowering beliefs within interactions in the Team is a form of coaching. We can do these internally and coach others. When we use these skills openly with colleagues we demonstrate our individual flexibility and willingness to find positive outcomes from all challenges facing the Team. We also help them to develop these skills as well.

The sorts of questions that we would need to ask openly are:

- What if we took the opposite view? Might we discover something that would improve our market share?
- Maybe the Reynolds Team is not acting out of aggression and as a prelude to a counterbid, but purely out of desperation.
- If we knew it was possible to reach that production speed, then what sort of action would we be taking now?

When we demonstrate these skills openly, we also demonstrate facilitation/leadership. At another level this also gives covert permission for others in the Team to use the same strategies. This then widens into a positive environment, open-mindedness and shared exploration of new action plans.

Overtly, these skills can be experienced within Teams through training workshops and coaching/mentoring with similar results – provided that the individual commitments are there and that the senior people in the Team manifest these skills and openness themselves. People feel encouraged to support managers who exemplify their own strategies. People are demotivated by those managers who tell others what they should be doing without following through by example in their own behaviours. Think of the cynicism that follows a political sound bite about using our cars less when you know that the politician making this statement travels everywhere by car and helicopter. Similarly, when a politician talks about the need to keep children in school during term time, having his own children miss the last week of term to go on holiday will lose him followers.

Chapter Five

Powerful Influencing

Leading and following

Summary

We are often in conflict with our self: part of us wants to do something, another part resists, and the effect is postponement or failure. These two parts are the leading and following parts, and, by diverting conscious attention to them both, we can improve our performance, success and self-confidence. This is powerful influencing of self.

How often have you wanted to achieve something but doubted or prevaricated until it has been too late to get much pleasure out of it anyway? It is like two opposing forces internally: one that wishes to take charge and take action, and a second that is less willing to follow. Here is the internal representation, or metaphor, for what happens in Teams as well. The fact is that, if we cannot lead and follow ourselves in the Team *inside*, what chance do we have of excellently managing or following in the real Team *outside*? Powerful influencing starts with our inner Team.

This perception of self provides another example of reframing those situations in which our individual performance is failing our own agenda. As usual, there is learning in this process. From that, the potential for new choices springs with motivated action and the subsequent satisfaction that comes from success.

Leadership or facilitation is just so much directionless wind unless the follower trims the sail and sets course. Our inner Team also needs to be motivated to ensure success. To do this, the leader/facilitator also needs an appreciation of the *follower's needs*. Understanding the needs of the follower makes it possible to set a direction/plan/policy that will *influence* the follower in an appealing way. If this is done well, the follower will be *motivated* (internally) to set about the task and succeed. Now *there* is a set of empowering beliefs!

Let's look at an example and some of the new tools available for taking care of our internal follower and making sure of our success. When we understand how this works internally, we gain insights about our colleagues, which helps us to understand and relate to them better. The spin-off from this is improved Team performance.

Paul wants to participate in an Italian course to give him some advantage when working with a new international partnership. He has already established the usefulness of the course both for himself and the Team. The course runs on Tuesday at lunchtime and will not interfere greatly with his work. But he misses two out of the first four sessions and the training and development manager speaks to him about this.

Two skills already explored that can make a difference in this situation are the prioritisation process (to decide which actions to undertake first – see Appendix 5), and measuring against the criteria for successful commitments (including confidence score) to check that there is the greatest possible chance of following his lead.

When Paul does this, he discovers that his confidence score is only 5 out of 10. He regards much of his normal work as *externally driven*. He feels that he must take action within set times to be responding professionally. He believes that if a task comes near Tuesday lunchtime, he must miss the course.

A reframing strategy (e.g. ask questions that increase understanding) might reveal a question such as this:

What if I am away or sick? Who covers my work then?

And a new set of possible actions follow naturally:

- I'll speak with Colin and Trudy about a rota of cover for Tuesday lunches.
- Wendy always plays netball on Wednesdays at lunchtime, so maybe she will cover me on Tuesdays if I offer to cover for her Wednesdays.

When Paul checks out his confidence score he sees that it has risen, but not quite enough to get him motivated and at the lessons.

Paul tries another reframing question:

What is the higher purpose or gift in this situation?

His experience (learning) may be that he has been somewhere like this before as a similar situation occurred at his last company. This may take Paul to a new understanding of his behaviours. He might check that his goal fits in with his ideas about his identity, purpose and values to see whether the part of him that is unwilling to follow may be encouraged by this insight. These strategies of thinking allow Paul new choices and better (self-) influencing skills.

Paul is still a bit stuck. His confidence score has increased but a part of him, his follower, is not quite certain that he is going to make Tuesday's class. Another strategy in this situation is called *chunking down*. It's a technique for finding out what is behind being stuck. The basis of it is another question: 'So, what stops me?'

Eliciting the follower's needs: chunking down

What happens when Paul uses this question to seek out more information about his reluctant follower within? Imagine this internal conversation:

PAUL: I'm still not confident that I will get to the Italian class more consistently. *So what stops me?*

PAUL FOLLOWER (PF): I'm slower than most to pick the language up.

PAUL: *So what stops me* picking it up faster?

PF: I need to prepare more in my own time, review past work, read ahead.

PAUL: *So what stops me* preparing more?

PF: Nothing now I think about it, but I don't want to appear a fool with other managers.

PAUL: *So what stops me* appearing bright with other managers at the classes?

PF: The same. Preparation.

PAUL: *So what stops me* doing that?

PF: Nothing – I only just thought about doing that!

Action can result from eliciting the follower's needs. Paul now has two linked actions: to catch up in his own time and to get to the next class on Tuesday. Returning to the criteria for successful commitments will tell him how likely he is to do those things. Of course, there is also a leader part of Paul that wants to do the Italian course. Maybe if that part of him were more compelled, then he might better motivate his follower to go along with the plan of action. To elicit some learning about this, we can introduce another strategy called *chunking up*. The eliciting technique involves another question: 'So what would/does that do for me?'

Eliciting the leader's motivation: chunking up

What happens when Paul uses this question to elicit more compelling information? Imagine this internal conversation:

PAUL: I'm still not confident that I will get to the Italian class more consistently. *So what would it do for me?*

PAUL LEADER (PL): I'd get more enjoyment from meeting our Italian associates and improved relationships with them. This could lead to more and better collaboration, which is a Team objective.

PAUL: *So what would that do for me?*

PL: My Team would notice my commitment to our objective and I would feel great about that.

PAUL: *So what would that do for me?*

PL: I'd just feel great, tingly all over. If a colleague said something about my commitment or my contribution to our Italian venture I'd be really happy.

The process elicits positive feelings for the leader within. From the self-coaching standpoint, it is a good idea to concentrate on positive outcomes – as opposed to negative outcomes that you want to avoid – since these are usually more motivating and provide definite focus for new behaviours. One way to do this effectively is to use some of the ideas explored with the timeline, as discussed above.

Positive feelings: making them more motivating

Earlier in the book, we looked at the use of logical (left-brain) thinking to prioritise a number of competing actions. Most of the logical processes ignore the fact that all of us have an emotional experience attached to our logical decisions (although we may not be aware of them). This is a fact of life in healthy, normal, human beings. Whether we are aware of these feelings or not, they will dictate how committed, motivated and successful we are. It is not absolutely necessary to be able to name those feelings, but it is useful to have an experience of achieving our final objectives in the present, since this will give us the motivation to succeed. If we have made a mistake and need to think again, then we will learn this too. Either way, we will find a route to success. In the timeline exercise, earlier, we used a set of questions to explore what it would be like to experience our objective as if it were happening in the present:

- How do I feel throughout my body?
- Where, if anywhere, am I tense?
- What quality does the light have?
- Are there any noises?
- Am I aware of my pulse or breathing?
- What is this experience like?
- What is happening around me?
- Who is here? What are they saying specifically?
- What else can I hear and see?
- Do I need anything else to make this goal a reality? If so, what is that missing piece?
- Is this goal significant and compelling enough for me to really *have to* achieve it?

The purpose of this trick is to have an experience that is as real as possible *now*. This experience should be compelling. In this way, it may work like a positive fix that one can safely return to when motivation is drifting. We are only human after all. But these strategies make sure that, in spite of ourselves, we still achieve our objectives!

Emotional experience attached to our logical decisions dictates how committed, motivated and successful we are.

When Paul does this, taking a sensory journey into his future, he finds a rush of pleasure from experiencing achievement in bringing the Italian partnership to new levels of trust and performance. His commitment and motivation are both high. Success is already assured.

Review

Let's review what we have covered:

- We found learning from the concept that there is an internal leader and follower in each one of us.
- Confidence scores using the criteria for successful commitments may increase after using the prioritisation process.
- It is useful to use two elements of reframing: asking questions that increase understanding and asking, 'What is the higher purpose or gift in this situation?'
- We examined the *chunking-down* process and how it elicits the *follower's needs*.
- We went through the *chunking-up* process to elicit what *motivates the leader*.
- To complete that positive state, we saw how asking timeline questions makes it more motivating.

A note on external Teams

These skills are just as useful in facilitating or managing others as they are in facilitating or leading our internal followers. An additional aspect to the processes of chunking down and chunking up is the idea of seeing a challenge in a big overview way (chunking up) or taking an idea or opportunity and getting more detail (chunking down) to explore how to achieve a possible objective. Within Teams, these processes also enable all individuals within the Team to contribute since individuals tend to have a preference for seeing the 'big picture' or for seeing small/detailed pictures (see Chapter One). Which of your Team members are the leaders and followers, and are these trends or task-specific? What would encourage the followers to be motivated? What is it they need in order to be more proactive?

Chapter Six

Internal Conflict and Dialogue

Summary

When we have internal conflict we have reduced effectiveness. Here we look at strategies for dealing with such conflict. If we are engaged in inner dialogue when we are with others, then we will reduce the quality of our understanding and limit the benefits that a higher engagement can bring to both ourselves and the Team. We look at a method for bringing the attention out again and methods for dealing with internal conflict.

In Chapter Four, we looked at an example where a manager had asked for a sales plan to be abbreviated, causing internal conflict in the writer of the plan. Communication and conflicts are both internal and external phenomena. Because of the obvious importance of communication in the Team context, we will need to look carefully at internal communication and conflicts and learn to handle these expertly. When we understand how to develop our internal skills, we learn and observe more about the skills of our colleagues and become more able to flex our tactics to provide better communication and reduce conflict. Remember that effective communication is not how and what you communicate: it is about the appropriateness of the communication to the listener.

Internally, communication dictates what we achieve, what we forget and where we fail. Failures are due to unresolved internal conflict, whatever the external situations. Again, we have an empowering belief. If we take on this belief then we take on responsibility and control for every situation. We will be more proactive in the Team. Efficiency will increase.

We will start, as in previous chapters, with the internal aspects before exploring in detail additional insights that have application within Teams. This should raise the quality of communication to new levels and deal with conflict effectively if and where it arises.

Communication and internal dialogue

We have experienced examples in earlier chapters of the usefulness of questioning in order to elicit new perspectives. There are real advantages to having structured internal dialogue. Many of us also experience unwanted internal cross-talk, which is less constructive. The internal critic may interrupt when we have better things to do, or when we have more important things to hear *externally*.

Here are some examples of the talk from the *internal* critic I refer to:

- It's impossible to do in the time … you can't do it … I can't do it!
- You said 'yes' but you don't even know where to start the project!
- What do you think you're doing?
- You're in it up to your neck now!
- He reminded me twice to complete the proposal by this afternoon and I haven't started!

Of course, there are many other types of internal dialogue, but these examples are some that illustrate internal communication that is limiting or taps into the realisation that we have taken on too much or are failing.

Many people go through their working lives with a constant barrage of internal dialogue going on. These familiar voices creep up on us, wasting time and destroying motivation. Apart from any other issue, in the moments that we are experiencing internal dialogue, we cannot attend to what our colleagues are saying. It's important, then, to have some degree of control over internal dialogue. Typical voices may include the following:

- She knows I can't get the report done by Thursday. She's testing my loyalty and commitment again.

- Roger's listening to this sales call. I'll trip up if I don't concentrate.
- Douglas is working late. Damn! I'm going to have to look busy and work on.
- Why doesn't she want the Bedford job? What's wrong with it? Hell! She asked me a question … what is it about … something about a meeting … which meeting?

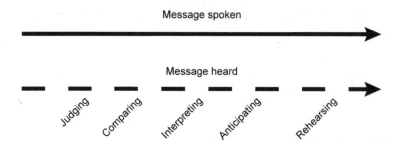

These internal voices tend to fit into one or other of five categories as shown in the figure. Some are judging, others are comparing or interpreting and sometimes there will be anticipation and rehearsing going on. All of these take our attention away from where it is needed. Instead of hearing the spoken message (top line) we only hear snippets of it (broken line). It is no wonder that some staff get so tired at work and their need for breaks is acute. A constant sequence of internal questions undermines self-confidence and makes for poor listening. If the internal dialogue is triggered because of self-doubts when with a colleague, the internal concentration reduces the quality of the communication. People notice, at some level, the poorer quality of attention, and they may respond badly. Internal dialogue can therefore result in a negative confirmation about the relationship and of our bad feelings about ourselves. It is self-fulfilling. But we do not *have to* run such patterns of thought. There are new choices available to all of us now.

We have already explored the use of questioning skills, which are part of the journey to breaking such patterns. By taking charge of our internal dialogue (in our own time) we are increasing our ability to notice dialogue consciously. This leads to the possibility of alternative choices and improved self-efficiency. Acquiring new habits of excellent listening enables us to intervene much more intelligently. This may be enhanced by feelings of self-trust; in other words, that we believe that by listening better, any response of our own is likely to be more relevant.

Patterns of negative internal dialogue

Some people may experience *patterns* of negative internal dialogue, by which I mean repeated episodes of self-doubt and self-judgment that are familiar in form.[8] Let's explore a strategy for changing these patterns.

Exercise

Recall one or more occasions when the pattern of negative internal dialogue has come to mind. Having done that, pick a particularly significantly example.

Mentally return to that time and place, and obtain as much quality information as you can about that specific experience. As you have done before, see what is around you, replay the voices, sense and experience what it is like. You will need to work with a score of 8 or higher (where 10 is your sense of the best possible reliving of that experience). Try to establish what the key external and internal points were at which things went negative (in other words the *trigger* of the negativity). These may have been internal or externally stated words, but could also have been an internal sense of dread or another uncomfortable state without recall of actual words. Invariably, there will be a change in your way of breathing in the early stages of the pattern.

Note this/these down here:

Internal and external triggers:

_____

_____

_____

_____

[8] Many people find it helpful to keep a special album in which they put positive stories, actions and feedback about themselves, sometimes with family pictures and feel-good images and triggers for positive feelings. Creating the album, maintaining it and carefully and regularly reading it (and attending to any warm feelings that arise) can help reduce negative internal dialogue.

If you have difficulty establishing the trigger(s), just relax – it is possible to continue this exercise without explicitly understanding the triggers.

Now I invite you to go outside this situation and imagine that you are a friendly observer. Take a good look at what is happening. Listen to what is being said. Make the experience of recall as perfect as you can.

What word or brief advice can you give that would make a difference in that situation? What other choices are there? Note these down:

Advice:

_____

_____

_____

_____

Choices:

_____

_____

_____

_____

There are two more steps. The first is to go back again to the same situation. Do this fully and as excellently as you can (8-plus), then receive the advice of the observer (from the above box). What choice can you now take in this situation? What may you do differently? Imagine yourself doing these things, and reach out for a positive difference from your initiative. Really develop a focus of attention around that difference and experience that fully before returning to the present. This step is best done three or four times until the receiving of advice and the consequence of it become fast and the positive difference is maximal.

The last step in the process is to go on a sensory journey. You will start by thinking of another future situation that may trigger a negative response similar to that already explored. I invite you to imagine yourself in that future situation fully. Experience it as if it were happening now. Having got to this point, and only then, accept the previous advice and notice any difference. If necessary, go over previous steps until the result is not only different but also very much more positive. As usual, check out your confidence rating for doing this when the time comes. If your rating is lower than 8, you may decide to go through the whole process again more slowly and with more repetition at each step. That is, unless the highest rating you can imagine is 8 rather than 10.[9]

Let's look at an example:

Peter and Tony have regular run-ins and these can be about almost anything. They work in an open-plan office and Peter finds that he looks to make sure that Tony is busy before going to the coffee machine so that he can avoid contact.

1. Following the procedure above, Peter takes his mind back to the last difficult interaction and recalls that Tony made a throwaway remark that was judgmental, and it was this that put Peter on his guard. Similar remarks had triggered the same reaction spontaneously.

2. Peter now takes on an observer position. He has a mental picture of himself and Tony and the situation. He hears himself saying, 'Yes, I'll discuss that with Bill and John,' and then Tony's reply, 'Haven't you got better things to do with your time?' Peter's insight is that Tony feels left out of Team situations and wonders about Tony's life outside of work. It occurs to Peter that Tony feels left out of the football activities that some of his colleagues do at weekends and that Tony may be lonely. Maybe if Peter involved Tony more, things would improve.

3. Peter recalls the same situation again. Instead of saying, 'Yes, I'll discuss that with Bill and John,' he says, 'Let's discuss that with Bill and John later – are you free around 3 p.m.?' Tony's reaction seems better.

4. Peter then imagines another situation in the future. Dialogue is going on and there is a point when Peter's natural style would be exclusive of Tony. He replays it with a new dialogue that includes Tony, and things go smoothly. In this imaginary case, the strategy worked perfectly. Following these insights, Peter included Tony (and other colleagues) more than he did and Tony has become more friendly and participatory generally.

---

[9] Remember, it is a fact that when asked what to rate 0–10, many people recalibrate the scale to suit their own nature. If your eight is your ultimate rating (equal to my 10), that does not matter, just as long as you compare your other ranking against the ultimate ranking and assess the significance of any difference between the two.

Internal conflicts

We already have a concert of strategies that can help in sorting out internal conflicts: questioning for greater understanding; questioning for higher purpose; the prioritisation process (where several options of priority exist); and so on. But what if the situation remains black and white?

For example:

'On the one hand, I want to do this work.'

'On the other hand I can't start it. It's too difficult!'

This example is a leader–follower issue in which the follower lacks confidence. The work may be vitally important but remain undone. One option may be to take the problem elsewhere in order to get external input – from a colleague or boss, for example. Another option might be to seek coaching/mentoring from them or to discuss other possible ways of achieving Team objectives with or without your involvement in the project. Before doing this, you may wish to check through the detailed example below, where Colin had such a dilemma and resolved it.

Colin has been asked to prepare an important marketing proposal for his company's main board. He has never done this before and the proposal is particularly important. His company has a single style for such proposals, which is detailed by up to four levels of structure in each and every section (of which there are many). Colin is a good manager and an excellent writer, but has creative flair. He was initially very pleased to be given the responsibility for the proposal. He now realises that the structure is onerous, specific in terms but vague in meaning (e.g. one section is called 'scope' and another is called 'overview' and there does not seem to be any difference). Colin feels that he cannot make an individual mark on the quality of the project. The covers, binding, typeface are all preordained.

The internal conflict is:

'I need to do this to satisfy my Team.'

'The task is confusingly structured and offers no prospect for personal impact or creativity.'

Colin goes through the process of chunking down to elicit the follower's needs ('What stops me?') and arrives at the two separate issues that stop him:

- understanding the terminology of the corporate proposal structure; and
- feeling that he has no opportunity for expressing his individuality in the proposal.

Colin can break the task into manageable bits, starting with reviewing other proposals to gain understanding. He may break the task down as follows:

- write down an overview map of the task;
- set down manageable time frames for each sub-task;
- pick an easy part and do it now;
- take a harder piece that will give personal satisfaction and do that next.

Colin can also ask questions to explore his choices:

- Could I look at other proposals to see what is expected in each section that I don't understand?
- Could I alter the balance, content and stress in each section to improve impact and make it more uniquely mine?
- Am I free to include visuals in the text or reduce text and refer to visuals in the appendices?
- Could these be in colour?
- Could my executive summary address the specific needs of the main board so well, and be so compelling, that the proposal has the highest possible chance of being taken up?

The end result of this may be viewed a compromise for Colin – but at least he was more likely to follow his lead and satisfy the Team. Below is another exercise that assisted Colin to reduce the conflicting dialogue in his head during his period of doubt.

Resolving internal conflict

Internal conflict typically has two parts. There is often cross-talk between these parts in a cyclical and unresolved dialogue. This is destructive and inefficient. Instead of oscillating between the two conflicting views, it is possible to change the experience of the situation and have a single learning experience. Conflicts need sorting. Internal ones are a good place to experience the compulsion of being free of conflict. Let us continue with Colin's example. He will be seeking to explore both sides of the argument, and the feelings or psychological state that they cause. Often these two sides crop up unwilled. In this exercise he will take control of each experience and in a final step have a first-time experience of holding onto both at the same time. The learning that comes from this provides an exit route from vacillating between the two arguments.

Colin extends one of his hands and, as he does so, he fully experiences that part of him that needs to complete the proposal. It takes self-discipline to stay with this part because the cycling of dialogue tends to be automatically triggered. Colin stays with the first voice and builds his experience of needing the proposal, accomplishing the writing of it and completing it in a way that makes his experience of it as real and positive as he can. As Colin withdraws from this experience he withdraws his hand also, linking the physical experience of extending his hand with the experience of completing the proposal. He repeats this several times.

The next part is the mirror image of the first, using the other hand. Colin extends the other hand as he fully experiences both the frustrations to his creativity and individuality. Again, he will repeat the process several times, withdrawing his hand as he withdraws from his experience.

Once Colin is able to do this easily, he may move from one hand (and experience) to the other, pausing to come back to the present state. He can check that he is fully back in the present state by asking the following questions:

- What is my full name? Spell it backwards.
- What address am I at exactly?
- How many colours can I see from here?

In the last step, Colin extends both hands slowly, switching his attention between states to have as full an appreciation of both of them as possible. His hands are kept sufficiently far apart to permit this sense of duality of experience.

Carefully and within his own range of comfort, Colin then brings the two hands as close together as possible – they may even touch.

Colin experiences a bringing together of the two states, providing him, for the first time, with a win–win feeling about the endeavour. The internal dialogue, which characterises internal conflict, is quiet.

Review

Let's review what we have covered:

- We looked at examples of negative internal dialogue.
- The importance of questioning for greater understanding was highlighted.
- We followed an example of eliciting triggers for negative internal dialogue.
- We followed a process for breaking repetitive patterns of negative internal dialogue, which involved:
  - isolating the trigger;
  - becoming the 'observer' and offering positive advice;
  - returning to the reference experience and accepting the advice;
  - thinking of a future situation that may induce the pattern;
  - introducing the advice into that situation;
  - checking that the confidence score for commitments is sufficiently high.
- We looked at breaking up tasks into smaller sub-tasks.
- Using Colin as the example, we went through a process of resolving inner conflict.
- We looked at a strategy for resolving conflict by producing a single experience to satisfy both needs concurrently.

A note on external Teams

Strategies for dealing with conflict within external Teams are covered in depth in the next chapter.

Chapter Seven

Conflict in External Teams

Conflict

Summary

We will look at conflict and methods that create wider perspective. These methods create fresh perceptions and increase choice of action. I provide strategies for resolving conflict issues. The practical use of belief is revisited and the language of conflict resolution demonstrated, including both the *broken-record technique* and *reflective language*.

Conflicts within Teams can be useful if managed well. This is analogous to customer-relations activities where complaints are turned around to such good effect that the customer ends up singing the praises of the company. Remember that all conflicts should lead to win–win components for each party, even if the trading results in a compromise where the benefit is taken later. *Both* parties need to participate in positive dialogue in order to get the win–win result – it takes only one party to jeopardise it.

We have been developing our understanding of people in previous chapters and this knowledge is an essential aspect of keeping healthy conflict from falling into destructive behaviours. But, if things do get out of hand, what else can we do?

In Chapter Two, I introduced empowering beliefs and gave the example of Jenny, who was having problems with a colleague called Sarah. The empowering beliefs used then were:

- Sarah feels intimidated by me.
- Sarah feels vulnerable generally.
- I do not have to get angry when challenged.
- Sarah is not trying to displace me or compete with me.
- Sarah would be much happier if I encouraged her more.

These provided insights, real or not, that made a difference to the next interaction that they had. Let's try another empowering belief that can make a difference, the belief underlying the 51 Per Cent Rule.

The 51 Per Cent Rule

The 51 Per Cent Rule is this:

In any given interaction, I am 51 per cent responsible for the result of that interaction.

The 51 Per Cent Rule eliminates the possibility of the following thoughts:

- I'm not doing anything now – he must make the first move.
- The guy is just a lowlife, I can't be bothered with him.
- He started it, so he must make it up.
- Without an apology upfront, I will not talk to him.

The example I am going to give is not a business one, but one that many may empathise with. My girlfriend had spoken sharply to me one evening when she was running me home in her car. There had very nearly been a serious accident and for a few seconds the headlights of a large van were heading straight for me. It was near my home and so there was little time to settle down and heal the situation before she dropped me off. She was in the habit of calling when she got home but did not call me that night. I guessed she was still upset. She didn't call the following day or evening either. It was only when I realised that the relationship was more important than the elements of poor relating in it that I was able to use the 51 Per Cent Rule. By accepting just a bit more than equal responsibility, it was clear that I would have to call her. I was sorry for not ringing and for reacting, in fear, the way I did in the car. I told her that. With no attack on her for her driving, I left a space in which, if she wanted to, she too could communicate. She took that option and expressed her regret about the poor turn. Up until then, she told me later, it had not even been a discussible issue with her. She was just too upset about my comment in the car. She had felt undermined. She also said she felt that I had hidden part of my personality from her and suddenly that the 'true me' was revealed – a familiar story in her previous relationships. The 51 Per Cent Rule works just as well in business situations as it does in domestic ones!

The 51 Per Cent Rule dictates that a stalemate cannot happen, since you do have a small but significantly larger responsibility for every aspect of the behaviours you are receiving from your colleague. Buying into the 51 Per Cent Rule ensures that you will never be in stalemate in this situation. Fifty-one percenters show initiative. Fifty-one percenters take action to heal the situation.

Acknowledge where they are coming from

The first step in a conflict interaction is to acknowledge your understanding of where your colleague is coming from. This may require a mental flexibility and great sensitivity if the conflict is deep-rooted. With luck, though, the conflict has more to do with opposing viewpoints than emotional mismatch and the mental trick will be without undue pain. Remember to consider getting in their shoes (or second-positioning – see below) and experiencing the observer state to get new perceptions and extend your choices of action (see below). Avoid value judgments and accusation completely. The purpose is to re-establish communication, not destroy it again! Once your colleague feels heard (and this may take several repetitions of the same simple sentences) you can then ask your colleague to work towards compromise or collaboration.

The broken-record technique

This technique is useful when you want to get a simple message across and also when a colleague is goading you to justify yourself in peripheral issues that do not immediately concern the conflict. Sometimes this happens when the event triggers off thinking about past events. These past experiences (with their emotional baggage attached) can cause the person to exaggerate the current situation, colouring it with negativity. The broken-record technique diverts attention from these peripheral issues. Simple repeated phrases could include the following examples:

- Do you agree that we should stay with the issue at hand?
- My reason for doing that was … I didn't realise the impact for you.
- I'm sorry that you're angry about that – it was not my intention.
- Do you think we can work towards a compromise?

The broken-record technique works by restricting the interaction to the issue. There may be several key sentences and questions that you keep coming back to without any deviation at all. This keeps both you and your colleague on track. The broken-record technique can also be used as a means of manipulation to incite frustration and anger. Beware of motives that are destructive! The technique is correctly used to bring a gift into the situation for *both* parties. Here is an example:

JOHN: The network went down for three hours last night because you didn't get the Dovedale switch fixed, as I asked. Now Wissick Supermarkets are threatening to move their account as we've crossed the six-hour downtime in one month clause, which breaches our contract with them.

BOB: I'm sorry but I'm not aware of any problem with the switches. The previous network drops have been due to cable damage and software failure on rerouting. Those are now fixed. I haven't been in touch with the current situation as I've been flying from Chicago and only just landed.

JOHN: The Dovedale switch isn't up to specification and you should have replaced it, as I asked.

BOB: I don't recall your asking me about the switch. Did you memo me or what?

JOHN: I asked you last week after the engineering-reports meeting.

BOB: I do recall the meeting but don't recall you asking me about the switch, but I'll look into it immediately. If there's a problem then I'll attend to it.

JOHN: That may not be fast enough. By the time you've researched the situation we may have more downtime, as we had with the relay centre last year. It's been a week since I mentioned it to you!

BOB: You're obviously very concerned about the downtime and I am also. I recall the meeting but don't recall your mentioning the switch. I'll look into it immediately. If there's a problem then I'll attend to it.

JOHN: Why don't you just order a new one now and arrange for it to be fitted now? This is serious.

BOB: I agree with you. It *is* serious. I'll look into it immediately. If there's a problem then I'll attend to it.

JOHN: Thank you.

Notice in particular the acknowledgements, such as, 'I agree with you,' 'It *is* serious,' and 'You're obviously concerned about the downtime and I am also.' The acknowledgements use the same words that they used to prevent any argument about semantic meaning.[10] These acknowledgements coupled with the broken-record technique prevent the conversation from getting sidetracked and bogged down in other sensitivities, thus increasing the chance of resolving the current situation. Follow-up would naturally include the earliest possible communication on progress steps and out-come. Future communication might include reports concerning reliability of switches. John therefore gains confidence because he is taken seriously and because his input has an impact whether or not these actions or reports would have happened anyway.

Experiencing their perspective

I have asked you previously to imagine that you are a friendly, detached observer in order to get some insight into personal issues. Where there are interpersonal conflicts, it can be incredibly helpful to use a similar method of thinking. In this new situation, the trick is to enter the mind and body of the person with whom you are in conflict to see if you can have a sense of their underlying issues. This can completely alter perceptions of what is going on and alter your own state so that the subsequent interaction is healthier. The perception may not be true. Actually, the truth is most often irrele-vant in these situations. It is enough to change your own thinking and act differently afterwards. These two spin-offs make a great difference in resolving conflicts.

Some time ago I was in a three-corner meeting with five people from three companies meeting as a group for the first time. My company was looking to take on the exclusive marketing and distribution of a range of products. The MD of the supplier seemed to be stuck. I guessed it was to do with a lack of certainty or confidence in the other parties' being able to do the job or maybe wanting to hang onto his 'baby'. I let discussion continue but took some moments

---

[10] I call this repetition of language *reflected language* and recommend it both in conflict situations and also where an individual is generally argumentative or sensitive to criticism. If you introduce a new word or 'interpretation' in these circumstances, there is likely to be an unwelcome response and the original issue will get sidetracked.

to try to *be* the MD. I imagined what it would feel like to be his age, to have accomplished what he had and to drive the car he did. Internally, I also adjusted my sense of my own body, *as if* I too were slightly slumped to one side, one arm stiffly reaching out to one knee, the other folded across my stomach. Suddenly I got an insight. I felt as if I really *were* tired of the whole business and wanted to get rid of the burden of it. I really hoped that I could be confident enough to let it go. I didn't want any more meetings, but this one was feeling like so many others. Would it go on and on? The result of this insight, whether right or wrong, was phenomenal. My words and sentences after this tended towards solving the unstated problem (as I perceived it). Within ten minutes the MD had made his decision to put all the marketing of all his product ranges with our two companies and he looked more alert and relieved.

If something is not working, why not try something different?

The essence of this technique is to get a different perception of what is happening in the conflict. It is a key element in conflict resolution in my work as a performance coach.

Exercise: Getting in their shoes

Try the process for yourself. Think of a situation that has given you a problem. Take your mind back to that place in all respects of sensing.[11] Imagine that you are this second person, complete with age, background, interests, responsibilities, reporting lines, body shape and posture, facial features and expressions, breathing patterns and way of speaking. The process of taking on these facts and experiences creates new perception. From this perspective, what does this particular issue mean? This may bring up a set of new and surprising ideas.

_____

_____

_____

_____

---

[11] It can be beneficial to move from one place to another as you go through the process of changing perception – a metaphor for the journey that is made in your mind.

For John and Bob, it may be that Bob feels the following when he experiences John's perspective:

- He feels desperate for a result.
- His feels his job is on the line.
- He feels threatened.
- He feels ignored.

These insights can lead to a different and more sensitive way of handling the situation. Once you see your colleague's sensitivities it is possible to hold off some of your own feelings in order to help the situation. As we have seen, this technique can be done in complete privacy away from the conflict and sometimes, as one becomes more expert, during the conflict. The instincts and perceptions that are gained do not have to be true. What matters is the new reality *as you sense it*. The resulting change in your state, behaviours, body posture and speech happen automatically. The result is always different from what would have happened otherwise. This is a gift in a conflict situation, especially if the issue is one in a recurring pattern of conflicts with the same person. An adage I often use in coaching is this: 'If something is not working, why not try something different?' This is a powerful tool for doing things differently.

Become an outside observer

We have just explored the process of gaining perspective by experiencing another person's perspective. Earlier we noted the potential advantage of being a remote and objective observer of self. Now, we can also use the observer situation to get to grips with the other person's perspective and imagine the conflict *as if* we were an observer, remote and safe from the confrontation. The friendly observer is watching, noticing and ready to give advice. From this position, it may be obvious that a few carefully reassuring words would heal the situation.

In the case of Bob and John, either of them could have used this technique after their difficult meeting to get insights into the situation. Thus, John, who had raised the complaint about the switch, might have an insight that Bob is overworked and stressed. John's insight might also be that Bob needs a more appropriate way of raising important issues rather than casually at meetings. Bob probably spends most of such meetings desperate to get away from them and back to the demands of a difficult job. John resolves to raise such issues with Bob on a one-to-one basis only. Bob's insights about John may be that he does not have enough technical and engineering information in his job to answer the immediate concerns of his boss at three in the morning. His boss was the head of engineering and hence has a very good understanding of all the technical issues in which John is unqualified. Bob resolves to filter through reviews and reports that might be of help to John.

Exercise: Observer Learning

When taking the position of an outside observer, work with your own senses. If you have a strong visual preference then you will be able to see the scenario – if auditory, then to hear it (for thinking preferences, see Chapter One). In any case, broaden your observation with the widest possible information that you have available. How cold is it there? What is the light like? What does the interaction feel like? Any insights and advice can be stored away while you continue to observe and gain further insights. As before, on returning to the position of your own self, take the observer's insights with you. Sense the difference that it makes to you. How would you do things differently now?

_____

_____

_____

_____

The last checks, as before, are:

1. Imagine the next future interaction (having this advice) and taking the actions that you have decided upon. Get a real sense of what that is like.
2. Check your confidence rating in being able to make any differences you decide on.

Review

Let's review what we have covered:

- Empowering beliefs can be used to gain alternative perceptions.
- The 51 Per Cent Rule states that in any given interaction I am 51 per cent responsible for the result of that interaction.
- We need to acknowledge where a colleague is coming from.
- We can use the broken-record technique to stay on track with the issue at hand. Reflective language reduces the chances of diverting discussion about the meaning of words and phrases (semantics).
- We can experience a colleague's perspective to gain insight about their mindset.
- Becoming an outside observer gives us insights into what is happening in poor interactions.
- If something is not working, why not try something different?

Chapter Eight

Communication Styles

Summary

Communication styles are often adopted patterns of behaviour that characterise how people choose to present themselves in the context of work, for example. They overlay thinking preferences, but are observable and can be measured.

In Chapter One, I highlighted that the quality of communication depends on its appropriateness to the audience for whom it is intended. No one would think to provide an overhead presentation for the blind chairman or spoken material for the deaf CEO of an organisation. Many presenters seem to believe that *their own* preferences in communication are the best. This view is both arrogant and ignorant. Understanding the thinking preferences detailed in Chapter One allows intelligent choices to be made about the way in which we communicate with others. It also highlights the pitfalls of making presentations that are geared to our own thinking. While the language used in a report may seem absolutely right and clear to you, it may be as clear as mud to some of your colleagues. Ability both to recognise preferences and to vary them is essential when you wish to appeal to the broad Team. Where the audience is unknown, using the widest possible range of preferences is necessary to maintain the best chance of keeping the interest and attention of your audience.

Communication styles have more to do with how people *present* themselves rather than with their *thinking* preferences. The most exaggerated styles often have their motivating origin in emotional characteristics, and as such are often seen as weaknesses. A complicating factor is that styles are often *adopted characteristics* rather than truly expressing an individual's nature. An example is the senior manager who always finds a disarming way to unsettle people at every first interaction. He may use a challenging comment or off-the-wall remark. Where this is an *adopted style*, the manager may be attempting to hide his inadequacy by trying to place people in a one-down position at every opportunity.

Communication styles are often *adopted characteristics* rather than truly expressing an individual's nature.

The point of detailing this and other examples is that, until now, we have been looking to understand more about ourselves and other Team members in order to communicate more effectively. Matching their thinking preferences has been introduced as a positive and useful tool in communication. Be wary, though, of matching communication styles! Being arrogant to match your boss may not be welcome! I am going to introduce a snapshot of styles that predominate in business, but it is not an exhaustive list. You can add many more of your own. In some cases matching may be appropriate, in other cases, as above, it is not.

Owning style

Some people like to have a sense of personal ownership in order to be motivated to act. Their sense of ownership may be a need for a *leading* rather than *following* contribution. Within the Team, the contribution that the person with an owning style makes may depend on his leadership of a project. And some managers need to reinvent the ideas of their colleagues in order to act on them. In some cases this reinvention is done without any actual change in detail whatsoever.

A university reader I knew was great at this, stealing ideas for himself and then giving them back proudly to his staff. He would even hear a joke and twenty minutes later relate the same joke back to the person who told him! In order to influence people with this style, it is helpful to feed them ideas without owning them yourself. Your reward has to come from the satisfaction of getting your policies carried out even though the kudos may be lost to you.

Contrary style

This may not be a style at all since people exhibiting a contrary style also tend to be mismatchers! However, there is a group of mismatchers who will not accept ideas and tend to go in opposite directions as a matter of habit. Influencing these types requires tact. I once coached the MD of a business whose CEO exhibited this style. The MD had already established some more or less successful strategies for getting policy past his CEO, albeit with major frustrations. One new technique, which worked for the MD, was introducing ideas with a negative bias:

- I can't see any value in this but thought that you ought to read it.
- The attached report seems of limited practical use. What do you think?

As the CEO operated from the contrary style he was certain to favour the opposite view and arrive where his MD wanted him! Although these types may appear to have little to offer Teams, their ability to look for alternatives can be creative and useful. The CEO referred to above leads a successful and fast-growing group of companies that grew and became dependent on technical innovation, although turnover of senior staff is higher than average for this industry!

Judgmental style

The judgmental style tends to be more limiting than the contrary style, because it derives from tenaciously held values and beliefs. People with this style say things such as:

- Marketing is a waste of money. We should spend more on selling.
- Women always take more time off.
- It's impossible to penetrate that market without a national trading company there.
- Networking the computer system will just waste our people's time. I can't support this proposal.

These individuals tend not to be very flexible in their thinking and the style is also not a great one for maintaining rapport in Teams. It is not a good one to match. Gentle challenges in the form of questions can assist people with this style to become more flexible in their thinking. Questions can be framed as below, but take care: this style is often accompanied by a fragile ego.

- That's an interesting view. Why do you think that?
- Did you read that somewhere?
- That sounds important. Who established that as a fact?
- What would be the benefits, then?

The beginning of change always starts with a challenge, whether from outside or inside – it is my belief that this is better done internally.

People with a judgmental style often have the thinking preference of internal reference (see Chapter One), and so it may take some time before gentle questioning results in any real integration of the questions. The more forceful the judgment, the more fragile may be the beliefs that drive the person. Gentle and consistent questioning can help people to reassess their beliefs. Beware, though: ensure that the questioning is gentle, or it may further polarise their position on any given issue.

Arrogant style

Here is another style to mismatch if you value Teams. Arrogance is invariably a very crude attempt to hide inadequacy – but it invariably expresses ignorance. People with an arrogant style often congregate because nobody else enjoys their company! They need an audience and so ignoring their trait can hurt them. Unfortunately, they developed the trait only because their skins are so thick, and hence may not even notice that they are being ignored. Giving them feedback probably won't help them, either. If you are stuck with someone like this in the Team, then realising that their behaviour comes from weakness rather than strength may assist you in dealing with any resentment or anger you may feel. It is best to get on with doing what you do well, develop your own skills and flexibility and not react to the arrogant style. Every opportunity needs to be taken to encourage the individual to acknowledge his style and its consequences within the Team. With careful handling and luck it may be possible to encourage the person towards self-development. Oddly, you may find that he craves praise even if he dismisses it. Acknowledging his strengths may assist the relationship, and, from a position of historical trust, enable you to encourage him to make changes.

Acquiescent and challenging styles

A challenging style is helpful in bringing new ideas into the Team. This is especially the case where the business needs to innovate to stay in the market. Some Teams are more open to challenges in thinking than others, and hence there is a need for the thoughtful, innovative manager both to match *and* to mismatch in order to provide new insights without stressing the culture unduly. The development of Teams that are fully open to new thinking and internal challenging is a journey. Most Teams get there by trains, some fly, but few rocket in their development. The beginning of change always starts with a challenge, whether from outside or inside. It is my belief that this is better done internally first in order for the Team to be fully prepared and effective for outside challenges. The first step on this journey is questioning. One person in the Team can start this process by asking questions like those dotted throughout this book. Questions demand a reassessment of held views, they demand new perceptions to be tried and they result in flexible thinking. These are all key elements of successful Teams.

Shy and assertive styles

Assertiveness is not the same as arrogance or aggression. It is the opposite of shyness. Neither style is right or wrong within Teams, and filtering out shy people reduces the talent available to us. What is important is that the Team should acknowledge the different styles within it and that it should encourage all within it to find expression for their ideas. This may demand flexibility about presentation. How many corporate meetings have an unwritten rule that agenda subjects should be introduced orally? A shy person may prefer to prepare something for distribution before a meeting so that discussion is general rather than centred on them. Flexibility is not just something we can do in our heads; it is something that should manifest in our organisations too.

Review

Let's review what we have covered:

- We established that a balance of matching and mismatching is useful and that matching thinking preferences is largely safe, whereas the matching of communication styles can be hazardous.
- We looked at a number of styles including:
  - owning
  - contrary
  - judgmental
  - arrogant
  - acquiescent and challenging
  - shy and assertive.
- We stressed the need for flexibility in our behaviour as well as in our thinking.

Chapter Nine

Assessing Motivation and Needs

Summary

We look here at needs and test our motivation for actions that arise from needs-assessment. To increase our success rate we check each motivation to establish the underlying or core benefit. We also establish working rewards based upon real desires.

Motivation is best developed by each person rather than by the company. The reason for this is that motivational factors are as varied as human nature. Carrots and sticks are only part of the solution, only part of the time!

I hope that you now understand more about your own thinking preferences, your communication styles and the choices available to you. I hope you also have a better idea about your ability to lead and follow yourself. With this background we are in a better frame of mind to paint a richer picture of our motivation needs.

Enjoyment, satisfaction and fun at work mean very different things to different people. For some, the idea that work ought to be enjoyable or fun is anathema. For others, these are essential ingredients for motivated work. This chapter is largely a workbook where you can build a detailed structure of your motivation. Does it arise from panic and stress, or from a focused desire to achieve? Is it consistent or do your motivational factors vary? What is the mix, and how can you ensure a balance in your existing job without needing to run elsewhere? Knowing and understanding your motivations allows you to take charge and satisfy them! Let's start, then, with an empowering belief, the presupposition that:

I am personally in control of my motivation and it is my responsibility to maintain it.

So many employees think that their managers should be able to peep inside them and discover what their needs are. Maybe it's a roll-on from that satisfying world of mums and kids. A wordless look or sulk and Mum knows what to do. Managers do that? Maybe! But what a difference an empowering belief makes! Now it's your responsibility. If your motivation is inconsistent and you want to change that, the following will help.

Exercise

Let's make a start! Write down the top five things that you feel motivate you to complete tasks successfully.[12]

Examples	Motivational factors
Stress! I've left it too late!	
I succeed	
Fear of failure	
1.	
2.	
3.	
4.	
5.	

In each case, use the leader or chunking-up question 'What does that do for me?' to elicit the core benefit (motivation factor) behind each motivation. Here is an example:

Stress! I've left it too late!
   So what does that do for me?

Gets me fired up, I get bored otherwise.
   So what does that do for me?

---

[12] I am not going to elicit motivational factors that do not actually increase performance. Some people may for example be motivated by the enjoyment of starting tasks and developing them but not actually completing the tasks. I will not attempt to explore this here, but other work, including internal and external conflict resolution described in earlier chapters, would be helpful in this case.

Makes me work efficiently – busy and effective, that's it!
   So what does that do for me?

Makes me do good quality work and achieve.
   So what does that do for me?

I feel great inside. Big, directed, happy glow and ready for the next job.
   So what does that do for me?

That really is it. A warm glow, directed, confident, ready for the next task.

All the steps are linked to the desired place of having done good work, having done it under pressure, efficiently, and getting the reward of feeling confident and directed. In this case, it is simple to make the link between the approach to work and the greatest rewards. In this case there is a need to schedule work to be started and completed just before it is due. This takes control and fits in with the desire to 'feel directed'. And there was no mention anywhere about money! What, I ask, does money do for you? Repeating the question leads to the core benefits. Now it's your turn.

For each of your motivational factors, use the question 'So what does that do for me?' to establish the core motivating benefit, and write it in the space below:

Motivational factors	Core benefit
1.	
2.	
3.	
4.	
5.	

If you have kept pushing yourself with the question and done it successfully, there is a chance that your five core benefits have reduced to just one or two. In any case, as above, make the link between your core benefit(s) and those factors and actions that will ensure that these benefits are a more regular part of your working experience. What do you need to be doing more or less of at work? What actions can you successfully commit to achieve those aims?

What I need to do more of is:

_____

_____

_____

_____

Actions therefore needed (specifically and within timescales):

_____

_____

_____

_____

Check your confidence score!

Maintaining positive momentum

When we try to make behavioural changes to create effective new patterns (and break the old ones), the process of learning and growth can sometimes take some time to become established and part of 'what you do'. Another issue is that of perception. If things seem hard there is sometimes a tendency to imagine that one's ability to make the change is not working, that one is failing, or it is simply too hard.

It is important to realise that this evolutionary period is normally cyclical in terms of motivation, as we can see in the diagram. At each period of doubt (downturns marked by circles) the person may well imagine that they have learned nothing, feel back where they started or will not be successful. At each awareness of these experiences it is important to assert that the downturns are a natural part of the learning process and that it is likely that, in fact, progress is still being made. With that mindset, it is likely that evidence for continued learning and aptitude is apparent.

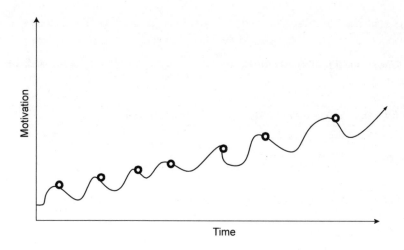

Needs and wants

Needs and wants are great motivators. If a given project does not have elements of these driving forces then it will be more difficult to apply ourselves to the job. A thorough understanding of our individual needs and wants gives us the possibility to adapt our thinking – and to make related decisions that *satisfy* those needs and wants. I remember the first time I was asked to design a training course for someone else. I immediately accepted because I enjoy creating novel training programmes. I soon realised, though, that the programme would not be my offering, and that I would not be getting direct satisfaction from running it myself. I got through it at the time, but it was difficult. Now I know that I would not have a difficulty about it. I realise that, although I enjoy writing for its own sake, I enjoy some sense of ownership in my creative work and also like to have feedback. By attending to these needs in projects I know that I have no difficulty in applying myself.

First, let's define the meanings of *needs* and *wants*:

- *Needs* are fundamental requirements for good health and efficacy.
- *Wants* are simple desires, which may or not be realistic.

Exercise

Now, try to categorise the examples below (although there may sometimes be grey areas!):

Example needs and wants	Need/want?
Regular human interaction	
Opportunities to review ideas	
Five times my current salary	
A personal assistant	
Faster computer	
Mobile telephone with lots of features	
More powerful car	

For some people, a more powerful car is a *need* – they do not feel confident without the obvious status symbol. In this case, the car should go in the needs category. For most of us a car may be a *want* but not fundamental to our ability to work healthily and effectively in a motivated way. We will concentrate on needs only here, as wants are of secondary importance.

Itemise your needs below:

My list of working needs	Extent of satisfaction
Minimum salary of …	

In the right-hand column, rate 0 (lowest) to 10 (highest), according to what extent these needs are already satisfied within your job *now*.

Take a look now at any low rates and see what has to change (internally and externally) to change that situation. To what extent are you in control of that situation and to what extent do you have to involve others? It may be that you need more feedback and recognition and have to seek more regular meetings with an immediate boss specifically to review your contribution and the effectiveness of what you do. You cannot guarantee the result of that request, but the first step is to take action and ask. And ask yourself, in this situation, what is in it for them and for the Team. As we saw with the 51 Per Cent Rule in Chapter Seven, it is important to take initiative for action rather than being passive and waiting for something on the outside to happen. Teams have to be productive, and your needs will not be on the agenda unless you put them there. Having made a commitment to action, remember to check through your criteria for successful commitments to be certain that these are actions that you will complete.

Dissatisfaction is sometimes due to employees not taking responsibility for their own motivation, and where external dialogue is required, due to their not taking the necessary steps to have that dialogue. There is a great deal of wind blowing about 'empowerment', but its most fruitful application is not by relinquishing responsibility downwards. It has to do with individuals being encouraged to develop their sense of responsibility for their work, their motivation and their communication. The corporate role is not to talk about it, but actively to promote it – and for managers to do it by their own example.

Rewards

The *wants* list is helpful for providing yourself with rewards for completing necessary work for which no obvious need is fulfilled. The level of reward has to be compelling enough to counteract any negative feelings about the task that has to be accomplished.

Jane was asked to spend three days at an exhibition, an activity she absolutely hates. Her feelings ran along the lines of finding another job, quitting immediately and going off sick. She may have been able to rethink her sense of the possible benefits in terms of her needs, but instead she went for the reward strategy. Each evening, after a day on the exhibition stand, she decided to eat alone, bathe and indulge a passion for champagne and chocolate. At the weekend she decided to revisit woods near where she had been raised as a child. She had not returned there for twenty years. Although the exhibition experience was psychologically a trial (and her feet hurt a lot), she got through the experience, albeit a pound or two heavier!

How do you know if the reward is suitable? It is helpful again to imagine the end of the task and what that will be like when the reward comes into being. If your gut feeling is, 'Damn it, no way!' then the reward is not enough. On the other hand, if the reward is compelling and you sense that you will be able to get past the job to the reward, then it will work for you.

Review

Let's review what we have covered:

- We wrote down our top motivation factors for our successful work.
- We used the leader or chunking-up question 'What does that do for me?' to elicit core benefits for each motivator.
- We checked through actions to improve motivation and provide motivating benefits in our work.
- We looked at the difference between needs and wants.
- We set down our fundamental needs for healthy and effective working.
- We ranked these 0–10 and highlighted those with low satisfaction in our jobs.
- We listed actions to set about improving the situation and checked all actions using the criteria for successful commitments.
- We looked at rewards based on *wants* to help get through tasks that are not compelling on their own merit.

A note on external Teams

It may seem odd not to provide you with an entire chapter on Team motivation. But I maintain that motivation is best developed by the individual. When these motivations are linked to Team goals, the potential for success by the Team is very considerable. Within Teams, then, workshops to explore and develop this thinking are recommended. Facilitation and coaching through internal (and external) conflicts that may arise at these workshops is a necessary support.

Motivation is best developed by the individual.

There are other things that Teams can do that are enabling for motivation. These include regular employee feedback and manager actions to agreed timescales. A completed agreement improves the manager–employee bond. Breaking an agreement is worse than not making one in the first place! Scope for individuality, expression and permission for people to 'fail and learn' are also helpful.

Where Teams are setting up new mission statements or themes it is important that these be fully developed and integrated throughout the Team. They should involve all stakeholders. Links between the Team goal and personal goals need to be established for every Team member so that each individual has a chance to buy into the statement or theme. In my experience, most Teams do this badly. In so many cases the themes are created in order for some top people to feel that they are managing creatively or to impress their board or shareholders. In the worst cases, one level down from the top there is no commitment to the theme in action (although there may be a lot of words suggesting that there is). In one example, a large US pharmaceutical corporation developed a new theme in which very few employees were involved in the US and none in overseas operations. Within a few weeks, many millions of dollars were spent on plastic cards, electric desk clocks and other mission-statement material. This was sent out to employees worldwide. The reaction in the US tended to be no more than a yawn. Overseas (where operations were being squeezed hard to support the stock market listing in the US), there was a negative reaction from the bottom, up to and including national VP level.

**Breaking an agreement is worse than not making one
in the first place.**

To a lesser extent, the same detachment of employees from mission statements and themes is found in the majority of companies. The main benefit of properly implemented themes is the training, facilitation and coaching that links personal outcomes to that of the Team, and the setting of agreed action plans with full employee commitment.

Chapter Ten

From Responsibility to Achievement

Summary

This chapter shows the important part that self-responsibility plays in achieving bigger and greater things. We touch on the methods that provide wider perception and that create a wider range of personal choices. Responsibility drives direction from choice to focus on a single strategy for success. Repeated successes create self-confidence and support the human instinct to achieve at higher levels.

Achievement derives from personal control. And personal control derives from responsibility. Without the ownership of problems and challenges that come from taking on responsibility, there is little chance of success. Responsibility may sound boring, but it is an essential key to performance psychology and to the development of individuals and Teams.

Repeated successes create self-confidence and support the human instinct to achieve at higher levels.

In the previous chapter, I suggested the empowering belief, 'I am personally in control of my motivation and it is my responsibility to maintain it.' This belief belongs in the mindset of an achiever. The 51 Per Cent Rule (Chapter Seven) is also a means to accepting responsibility for a situation. Up until now I have tried to avoid the word *responsibility*, but now we must face it directly. Taking responsibility works! Here are some more beliefs that may be helpful:

- I am responsible for my job and my future in this Team.
- I have, or have access to, the resources I need to accomplish my role(s) excellently.

- When I establish my personal control in a situation, I have maximum effectiveness.

Each of these beliefs may be read, understood and then mentally taken on board to make a difference.

Let me introduce some of my thinking about fate and destiny, which are characterised by the difference between irresponsibility (which puts achievement in the realm of chance) and responsibility (which provides the opportunity for success).

Fate

A belief in fate is a belief that 'everything is preordained'. I heard of the son of a leading physician who held this idea. He carried with him two dice which he used in order to decide what action he should take whenever he was uncertain of what to do.

Since he, too, was a medical doctor, this strategy was unfortunate for his patients! His dependence on the dice increased in tandem with his increasing uncertainty. Since he was focusing on uncertainty, it is no wonder that he became better at achieving an uncertain state of mind excellently! I am not sure whether he survived (or, indeed, his patients survived) or whether he now languishes in an institution throwing his dice to determine whether to have his tea immediately or later. Similarly, I knew another person who had given his responsibility to God and cheerfully continued through amber traffic lights in the belief that his family's death is God's responsibility and not his. Needless to say, I do not travel with them any more! God may have an impact on our spiritual growth, but it is mortals who decide whether to cross the road or not.

Fatalistic approaches are not often exhibited in Teams but do prevail to a lesser extent in some individuals. Here is an example of fatalism in the comment of a group sales director about a failed sales drive:

'Well, we gave it our best shot, but sometimes that's the way it goes.'

He was not challenged for saying this, and I was too young and inexperienced to take him up on his limiting belief at the time. By giving away the responsibility for the sales drive to chance (or fate), he and the company gave away the opportunity for learning, too. No moving forward, no improvement in success rate. A less fatalistic (and more successful) sales director might have said:

'We screwed up. Costs are higher than net gain and we're 70 per cent behind budget and 76 per cent behind target on this range. I'm already investigating what went wrong so that all my Team learns from the mistakes made. This is a major disappointment for me and one for which I accept full responsibility. At least I will make sure that our future campaigns will not fail for any of the same reasons.'

Destiny

My sense of individual destiny within Teams is that there are ideal tasks and goals that, if recognised, provide the individual with the greatest possible satisfaction and success. If these ideal tasks and goals can be recognised then they are of ultimate and continuing benefit to both the individual and the Team.

Choices are merely ideas if we do not have the courage to explore them.

What needs to be in place for us to recognise and act upon the wide range of possibilities circling around us?

By now you already have many of the components in place, such as a clearer understanding of your preferences and a more excellent way of organising and prioritising your actions. If you have taken on the suggested empowering beliefs, then you are also feeling comfortably responsible, in control of your future and confident of achieving the detailed actions that you have committed to so far. Destiny provides us with potential by way of options. Self-knowledge and growth give us the skills to take the options that will provide us with the best possible satisfaction and success. A range of options becomes a set of choices only when we empower ourselves to be able to explore any of those options if we choose.

Choices are merely ideas if we do not have the courage to explore them. We return, then, to the need for responsibility to be coupled with self-permission to create motivation, proactivity and achievement.

Perceptions and choice

New perceptions offer new choices. Your new perceptions can come from timelines, from becoming an outside observer and/or from experiencing the perspectives of others. They may also come from asking yourself questions that offer greater understanding or that specifically probe what the higher purpose or gift in a situation might be. All of these techniques offer new perceptions, which provide more choice.

Choice and control

Realistic choices allow you to feel in control. Instead of feeling relatively powerless in the absence of choices, suddenly you have new ones. You exercise judgment, establish action, check that the actions are realistic and that you have the necessary criteria for successful commitments to ensure action. You are empowered to act in keeping with your needs and motivations.

Control and achievement

The personal control expressed in setting new actions provides confidence and conviction. The chance of success is now established as part of your choice about your destiny, not simple fate. The freedom and sense of self-permission that this engenders is wonderful.

Achievement breeds further achievement

Once these steps are taken, the prophecy is self-fulfilling. Achievement follows achievement as day follows night. Repeated successes raise self-confidence and you find yourself achieving more and more. For those that have inner doubt and inner dialogue, repeated success helps quieten the voices.

Acknowledgement

It is critical to pause after our achievements and reflect on our decisions, our bravery, our success.[13] If we do not do this we do not get the full and enduring benefits of self-esteem. It is possible to rush from one success to the next and burn out, and I can think of one friend who did this and ended up a suicide. Acknowledgement might have saved him.

Review

Let's review what we have covered:

- The difference between fate and destiny is the difference between irresponsibility and responsibility.
- Responsibility provides the driving force to seek alternative perceptions.
- New perceptions offer more choice.
- Selecting a choice and making commitment to action maintains personal control.
- Personal control provides the best opportunity for personal achievement and self-confidence.
- Acknowledgement is vital in building self-esteem.

A note on external Teams

You will have heard the old adage that 'an offence may not be given, it can only be received'. This is an excellent example of reframing. Once you accept this idea (if only temporarily), you are provided with a new perception about the situation and

---

[13] McLeod, 2007.

potentially a different outcome. Here is a new one that I offer you:

Responsibility cannot be given: it can only be taken.

If this is true, how might we stimulate the highest possible commitment to responsibility in our staff and encourage success?

One way would be to make sure that we are doing the following:

- Do not attempt to give responsibility.
- Discuss the possibility of its acceptance with the intended recipient.
- If realistic, discuss this in a wider forum with other Team members so that other allied skills and abilities can be brought to bear on the objective.
- Do not simply *expect* commitment, but check for it by discussion and by asking questions.

Some good questions to ask are:

- What are the benefits of this task to Team objectives?
- Do you need other resources to accomplish the task?
- What time commitment and what time frame are necessary for completion?
- Have you included enough time for those steps that are not within your control?
- What is your confidence level that you can do this in these timescales?
- Are you in control of all the steps?
- What is your commitment level?
- What will you personally experience by fulfilling this task successfully and on time?
- Can you imagine having done that?
- Is there anything you could do that would add to your feeling of satisfaction?

This is a basis for providing an environment where success happens in the Team. It is not a prescription. It is important to redraw these guidelines in order to include language that is aligned with your own Team culture.

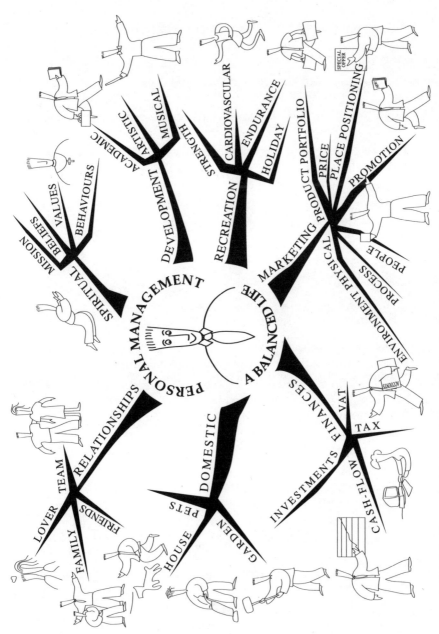

Revisit the map at intervals in order to check out new directions (see page 118)

Chapter Eleven

Objectives and Action Tasks

Objectives and action tasks

Summary

We already have a good set of skills, understandings and insights to structure our success more excellently. In this chapter we will do some more checks to find the links between our personal agenda and Team ones. We will go through a checklist of tasks that form part of a personal success strategy. The detail depends upon your input, since these tasks must conform to *your own* preferences and styles. From this you will develop new structures and methods that suit *you*. This will be more motivating than drawing on a galaxy of solutions that do not necessarily fit your personal requirements.

This chapter is written as if you were progressing towards a big goal through a number of smaller goals. However, many of the action tasks introduced are relevant to individual goals – in particular, the checking process for alignment with Team goals! Please pass over those that are not relevant to you at this moment. If you do not have a big goal to head for now, then you may decide to try out the process for a smaller goal or objective.

For each objective, you need to check the criteria for successful commitments (see page 26). The first criterion is that you are in control of the outcome. If, for example, you are a junior sales manager and your objective is to be CEO in ten years, the criterion is not satisfied. Such an objective or goal needs to be broken down into realistic objectives, complete with milestones and time frames. In this chapter, we are looking principally at objectives that do meet the criteria. These objectives will be those for which you already have a good level of both confidence and commitment (following the techniques developed in earlier chapters).

Timeline to the future goal

I suggest that you use the timeline technique to explore the choices, decisions and circumstances that you perceive will get you to your goal. Having done this, you will need to explore the steps along that timeline in more detail. The experience of that goal needs to be very compelling. Full exploration of the steps helps to focus on issues, limitations and strategies for success in order to achieve the goal.

Setting out steps

The paths to a greater vision may be numerous, but we may miss opportunities along the way if we have not explored all the possible routes to getting there. For this purpose, it may be best to review the steps as if you are a detached observer in order to use logical, dispassionate thinking and to see yourself objectively. From this new perspective, ask:

- What is this person like?
- What skills does this person have?

- How does this person fit into the Team?
- What contribution does this person make?

Having set the scene in the 'observer role', try to stay logical and dispassionate in broadening the understanding and choices available at each step to the big objective. Key questions might include:

- What other routes might this person take?
- Would it be best to get additional experience and training along the way?
- What further skills and experience does this person need?
- What steps are necessary to get those skills and experiences, and in what timescales specifically?
- Why will Team members have confidence in this individual?
- What sort of things will they be saying about this person?
- What special qualities will make the difference in reaching the objective?
- How will these qualities be developed?
- Are matching qualities fully developed and appreciated by those who decide?
- If not, what can be done to improve this situation?
- What about personal appearance? And is this aligned and appropriate with each step?
- Which behaviours need to be enhanced or changed at each step?

Testing out transitions

The points of change or transition are especially important. It is at these steps or transitions that mindsets need to be re-evaluated and changed if necessary. Questioning skills are the key to this. Again, step into the role of an observer to get an objective, logical perspective on these questions:

- How many different scenarios are there for the opportunity to arise?
- What are they specifically?
- Who are the key people in the decision-making process?
- What will they say about this person?
- What could be done to improve that more quickly?

- How could key qualities be more obviously demonstrated faster?

It's possible that drawing a mind map[14] showing the interconnecting steps and alternatives would assist in the development of these ideas, since there will be numerous steps that need to be explored and links made. The mind map will help to make actions clear and an example is provided (see page 113).

The first step or steps are the ones that are essential now. Check the criteria for successful commitments to be sure that your commitment is certain.

Your perspectives of the map and your development and understanding will change constantly. Teams grow and change too, as do opportunities, so it is necessary to revisit the map at intervals in order to check out new directions.

Checking alignment with team goals and qualities

The Team may not have detailed goals, but that will not matter, since you can set these down yourself from your current understanding. If we have a good idea about how our own objectives fit those of the Team, then we can adjust and make changes, spot possible pitfalls and plan to avoid them. Knowledge is power! The next exercise is set out to do just that. Follow the example.

Kathy is in telesales. Her first-step goal is to convince her manager that a training course would be useful in developing her sales ability.

Kathy lists what she understands the Team's top five goals to be. In the next column (C) she then ranks what she feels the training course will contribute to those goals (0 low, 10 high). In the next column (K) she sets down the level of her own motivation or alignment with the Team goals. From these two sets of rankings, Kathy can then work out her own potential match with Team goals by

---

[14] See for example, Buzan (2006).

Team goals or team quality	C = Contribution of training course to team goals	K = Kathy's goals	C × K	Maximum possible C × 10
95 per cent return of calls within 10 minutes	6	0	0	60
120 calls per day	10	0	0	100
Sales of 3,000 items per week	8	10	80	80
refusal rate below 1 per cent	4	7	28	40
call terminations = zero	2	6	12	20
		Totals	120	300
		per cent of max	40 per cent	

multiplying C and K. The last column shows the maximum alignment scores that someone could achieve (C × 10). From this, a percentage can be worked out by multiplying the first total by 100 and then dividing it by the second, bigger figure. In Kathy's case this is 120 × 100 divided by 300, or 40 per cent.

Exercise: My goal alignment with team goals

Now set down in the left-hand column the top five Team goals and qualities that are key measures of the Team's success as you understand them.

Team goal or team quality	TR = Team rating	A = My goal: alignment rating	TR × A	Maximum possible TR × 10
		Totals		
		per cent of max		

Next, for each of the Team goals, place a Team rating (0–10, where 10 is high) for how important you think the *Team* holds that Team goal. This now illustrates which goals are most important to the Team.

In the next column ('My goal: alignment rating') place a figure for the contribution that your first step or steps make to each of the Team's goals/qualities, again 0–10. Already you may have an idea how well these match Team criteria, but you can continue with the scoring process to establish an actual percentage measure of that alignment.

The next column will be the product of multiplying these previous rankings together (row by row). This new score gives an immediate measure of your alignment to Team goals for each Team goal. These can be compared with each other to find your greatest strengths and weaknesses.

For any given personal goal it is now possible to establish a quick measure for assessing its contribution against Team goals and key qualities. If it scores badly, you may want to lower the priority of that goal and raise the priority of a goal that is more closely aligned to Team goals. If it scores well, the evidence for alignment with Team goals may give you greater encouragement to carry the goal out.

Logical procedures do not take account of feelings (which are powerful motivators and demotivators). After computing the process, it is useful to take time to reflect and sense whether the result is right for you. You might consider this your 'gut feeling'. If the goal is not aligned with your gut instinct, then it may be necessary to look again at other options that are more closely aligned with both personal and Team goals.

Structuring tasks for success

How should you best set out your action tasks? Look first at your preferences. If you are particularly visual, you may want to set out your tasks as coloured pictures on a wall chart. If your creativity score is high, you may want to use stick-on shapes that you can move around. If you are especially auditory, you may want to record the tasks on tape and play them back while travelling or while at home. If very kinaesthetic, then think about using cards for each step and sorting them out into order by physical movement – this may be a more stimulating and memorable way to set out the tasks.

Discipline and responsibility for your goals dictates that you will need to set adequate reviews for yourself using a calendar, diary, wall chart, software program or other appropriate means to remind you. A particularly useful empowering belief to adopt is this:

Changes to steps and milestones are sometimes necessary.

Prioritisation often has to change in real working environments. Many people associate such changes with failure, and this negative mindset means that the next goal will also have an increased chance of being missed. Pre-adjusting your mindset to accommodate such changes positively can make the difference between failing and succeeding.

Reward setting

Your preferences for setting milestones and the means of carrying them out on time need to be individual, as highlighted above. An additional factor that may assist you is the setting of personal rewards (for meeting your tasks fully on time). We looked at rewards earlier and the importance of making sure that the reward is sufficient to act as a working incentive. The bigger the task, the bigger the reward. The Team and management are not always there when you complete your tasks; hence these personal rewards are a way of compensating for lack of external acknowledgment. For many people, the external acknowledgment is less important than the internal. But internal control can help you stay ahead of the expectations of the Team. By attending to personal goals and setting a realisable agenda you accomplish them within your own timescales, rather than those set for you. This process means that the Team is always very comfortable with your effort and satisfied with your contribution.

Review

Let's review what we have covered:

- Big goals need to be broken down into smaller goals.
- The use of timelines helps to explore the journeys to the ultimate goal.
- Review the steps from the 'friendly observer' position, using questions.
- Include questions about significant people, choices, skills and experience.
- Use the observer position to examine the transitions where change may occur.
- Ask questions from this perspective to gain information, learning and more choice.
- Mind-mapping is an example of a way to set down the many paths visually.
- Identify the first step(s) within your control (criteria for successful commitments apply).
- Use the checking system for rating the importance of your first task(s) to the five principal goals and qualities of the Team.
- In setting tasks and timescales for the task(s), incorporate personal thinking preferences.
- Use personal rewards as incentives for achieving tasks on time.

A note on external Teams

It is useful for Teams to have new ideas about the way that they set tasks for themselves and manage those tasks. Most appropriately, training should encourage personal adaptation so that any systematic process is unique to each individual, even if progress reports are necessarily more uniformly formatted. Individuals in the Team have inherent preferences, and the closer their system fits in with those preferences the greater the likelihood that they will use their system – and use it effectively! Arbitrarily adopted management systems are good for only some of the people, some of the time. In fact, they are ideal only for the person who created the system!

Chapter Twelve

The Coaching Culture

Summary

The tools and techniques that have been described and illustrated in the book so far are all those used in coaching. This chapter makes this learning overt in the context of both the disciplines of practical coaching (whether informally or by formal arrangement) and in creating the *coaching culture*. The Appendices include further information about mindsets for coachees and coaches.

Almost everything that we have done so far can be summed up in two words: *internal coaching*. As I hope you have discovered, the techniques are simple and involve being positive, using questions for greater understanding, exploring new perspectives (including the friendly, detached observer) and the use of timelines. And, as good coaches do, we also check out our commitments, ranking and prioritising goals to establish progress against set timescales and with appropriate rewards.

The results are simply stated, too: greater perception, increased choice, improved management.

Managers are released from managing most of their people if staff are skilled and have adopted coaching styles.

The application of these techniques within a Team and between all members of that Team constitutes some of the key elements of the coaching culture. A coaching culture is one where individuals move fluidly from learning to informing and questioning and back again. Individuals take responsibility for their own learning goals and motivations.

So what would we be saying about a Team that has its coaching environment fully established?

- The Team is open to challenge and is flexible.
- The Team is self-challenging; indeed, its challenges are more internal than external.
- The Team is ahead of the competition.
- The Team is innovative.
- The Team is superbly supportive.
- Team members are mentoring each other to new levels of performance.
- The Team has a 'we can do' philosophy.
- The Team members are all committed to encouraging the best from themselves and their colleagues.

Teams like this are top performers. Interestingly, all the above could also be said of the so-called *learning organisation*. The coaching environment is an all-pervasive and nurturing element that creates the learning organisation. The only significant difference between the coaching culture I have described and the learning organisation is the extension of the culture of coaching into associated Teams (both within and *outside* the host organisation).

The first criterion of coaching culture within Teams is:

All individuals within the Team are both coaches and coachees, and each individual demonstrates his or her ability to switch between roles instantly and seamlessly.

Some thoughts for management

Managers are advantaged if they make a conscious decision as to whether they are managing from outside the Team or as an integrated part of the Team. There are distinct differences in style depending upon the manager's mindset. My view is that the Team is more effective when everybody in it, including the manager, is pulling together. Pushing should not be necessary in a functional Team, as Team agendas are clear and the individuals will take (and be encouraged to take) personal responsibility for establishing their own goals and motivations. This will enable the Team goals to be met to agreed timescales. The coaching culture is not a strategy (or this year's idea). It can be fully embraced and fully effective only where everyone within the Team demonstrates the culture through his or her own behaviours.

The Team will be stronger and more powerfully successful if it includes the manager as well. Managers are released from managing most of their people if their staff are skilled and have adopted coaching styles. That means that managers can do more of the strategic thinking that can lead to quantum changes in efficiency. Naturally, in a coaching culture, the origin, testing and prototyping of new initiatives is likely to come from several origins, not just the manager. This harnessing of minds can often create solutions at a more significant level of change and productivity. Not only that, such solutions are not resisted but eagerly incorporated.[15]

Review

Let's review what we have covered:

- The exercises in the book so far are a significant proportion of the skill sets needed to coach others and those of us in the Team.
- A coaching culture creates top-performing Teams that are flexible and creative.
- The coaching culture is the key element of the learning organisation.
- Management must decide whether it is a part of the Team or not. If so, then it must exemplify the coaching qualities of that culture.

---

[15] See, for example, HelixSys, which is the structured corporate-change model of 3CCCs that involves all stakeholders and is a significant adaptation of Otto Scharmer's U-model (www.3cccs.com).

Conclusion
Open Minds and Flexibility

Any single individual within a Team will influence and encourage other Team members by using the skills detailed in this book. Clearly, it is advantageous to have total Team cooperation together with a training-and-development effort that encourages the coaching culture. In their absence, your own efforts will be rewarded in any case. Remember, cultures are characterised by matching behaviours. Another great mechanism for individual and Team learning is feedback and training, which should be directed at successful appreciation and use of feedback. In the Appendices, I include a model of feedback that is successful.

The skills in this book enable you to have more choice about where you match and mismatch in your chosen Team. Let's list some of the words that might describe the behaviours and skills that you could exhibit:

- open
- flexible
- supportive
- listening
- responsive (to feedback)
- constructive
- creative
- inspiring
- reflective
- leader
- achiever
- realistic
- perceptive

If people are using these words to describe you, the chances are that they will also be matching some of your behaviours too. Matching behaviours constitutes a culture. Your effort can therefore help the success of your organisation in a measurable way.

I include the descriptor *reflective*, since much of our most significant learning happens in the spaces between thinking. Reflection is not just making space for thinking and strategic thought: it is about silence and the miracles of perception and understanding that take place in that reflective space. To grow, to change, to lead and increase our performance and influence in the world, we must be more reflective and respond positively to feedback, however it may be intended!

In so many organisations we have the culture of the bully and the neglectful. In so many organisations there are glib 'values' that are meaningless mumbo-jumbo and alienate the Team from management. There are so many managers who talk about openness and flexibility but do not demonstrate it themselves. And there are managers who talk about vision and values but have no sense of Team, and then wonder why their performance falls short before they embark on the next expensive 'theme'.

So often, training and development is something we *do to* the staff, not something we are fully part of in management. Management programmes are often divisive, further establishing the difference between the staff and the management. Here, then, is the basis of a programme for real change for the entire organisation. In order to achieve that we bring together these same core skills and abilities – they not only support *the idea* of Team, they *create* Teams. Tomorrow's top performers are embracing these skills now.

Reflection is not just making space for thinking and strategic thought; it is about silence and the miracles of perception and understanding that take place in that reflective space.

It remains true that organisations are only as good as the individual qualities of their people and their ability to harness these into clear objectives. And there are two extremes of thinking of how best to do this. Both are seen within sales management in particular. In some companies it is normal to hype up the competition between individual sales people by rewarding best results and establishing a separation between the best and the less good performers. This creates pressure from top to bottom, which can appeal to those attracted to operating *away-from* strategies – that is, *away from* failing. The carrot-and-stick approach does work, but in many Teams the stick is too uncomfortable and turnover is high, and that means that management tends to reduce its investment in HR even more. The stick also encourages competition to the extent that many in the group will not share best practice and may not encourage others – hardly what modern leaders would call a 'Team'! Most managers would agree that the sales people should operate principally *towards* strategies in a *towards* environment. Failure to do this results in ambivalence about both (unsupportive) colleagues and about their management. The Team typically remains fragmented, with smaller (supportive) subcultures developing within the organisation. Staff turnover and absence are often high.

Other sales managements are set up using *towards* strategies only. These managements support and encourage those who are doing less well in each time frame and remain focused on objectives that are realistic. I leave it to my readers to decide which makes the more effective Team and produces the better results. Of course, these stress factors are not isolated in sales!

Some clues to the nature of an organisation can be found in notices, codes of practice and operating procedures. If the language is full of 'do not' rather than 'do' you have a crude measure of the extent to which the organisation is strategically 'away-from' or 'towards'. I believe all this material is best couched in language that informs about expected behaviours rather than dwelling too much on those that are not. As a basis for performance review and underpinning positive culture, such messages play a significant part.

The word *Team* is used generically to describe any group of people in a department, division or company. Hence, those of us in Team development have had to differentiate by adding superlatives, The super-Team, top Teams, high-performance Teams, and so on. A Team is most definitely a group of people. And they should be pulling in the same direction if they are worthy of the term *Team*.

In Teams, there is a definite pervading culture, based on key elements of matching, that characterises that Team. The best Teams are growing and evolving to move with changes outside and inside. And the keys to that ability to change are open-mindedness and flexibility. With these two characteristics developed in every individual, anything becomes possible. I hope that this work helps my readers go still further in both those qualities than before. Now is the time to fly.

Appendix 1
Feedback

Feedback is a very significant stimulator of learning and change in individuals and Teams. To be most effective, the individuals must all respond well to feedback and the feedback needs to be usefully given.

Feedback challenges the way we think, who we believe we are and the effects we have in the world around us. When we provide good feedback we give the same possibility for reflection and growth to others. Part of the training and preparation for giving and receiving feedback is positive mindsets in both the giver and receiver. The following two Appendices will provide trainers with a helpful platform of ideas about how to set up appropriate mindsets for that.

At one time it was recommended to sandwich feedback between two 'positive strokes' to support the rapport and make the feedback more palatable. But without modern practices and aptitude in giving feedback, what was given was often quite indigestible! The sandwich should be unnecessary. I recommend feedback given as follows.

- Describe what you have noticed (behaviours) in factual terms that can be observed and measured.
- Illustrate what the effects those behaviours have in factual terms and include (if you are comfortable with this) any emotional reaction of your own (only) to those behaviours.
- Describe the specific behaviours that you would like to notice in any specific context(s) and the effects that you believe that would have (including the ones you know about – your own expected reactions).

Here is an example:

John, when you tap your pencil during a meeting as you did just now and in Tuesday's project meeting, it's distracting to me, and I wonder whether you're really listening to what's being said. What I would prefer to notice is your pencil left on the table and your obvious attention and interest to what's happening in the room. If you did that at our next meeting I feel confident that I'd be much happier with your presence in meetings.

Appendix 2

Qualities and Mindset of the Coachee

It is not just the coach who needs a clear mindset in a coaching situation. It helps if the coachee also has a clear mindset. Empowering beliefs for the coachee might include the following.

- I value challenges.
- I value different perceptions.
- I value my colleagues and myself.
- I believe that:
  - challenges bring me opportunities for new perceptions;
  - all the Team have perceptions and mindsets that offer me learning and increased effectiveness;
  - I have perceptions and mindsets that offer my colleagues learning and increased effectiveness;
  - the Team and the individuals are phenomenally successful when embracing the coaching culture;
  - feedback from a coach is valuable because it invariably contains learning; and
  - coaches and coachees both learn from their interaction.
- I can be both coach and coachee, flexibly moving from one role to the other.

There are 'givens' that fall from each statement. For example, if coaches and coachees both learn from the interaction, it is not a one-way track, and there is no one-up position in being either coach or coachee.

Another example is the idea that feedback is valuable. This belief then extends even to that dialogue that may contain negative value judgment (which it shouldn't): 'You are not shaping up, James.' The learning comes from exploring the statement. For example, it may show that the person saying it *cares* about the situation or they would not bother to say it at all. If they care, then they are likely to continue to support and encourage James to 'shape up' if that is necessary for him, for the Team and for the relationship.

I encourage you to go through each of the statements above. As with the examples, please look for the positive learning that arises from thinking them through. This is an exercise in openness and flexibility and a test of your ability to find new perceptions through self-challenge. Each of these qualities is as important to the coachee as to the coach.

Appendix 3

Qualities and Mindset of the Coach

Empowering beliefs are a good place to start in establishing a healthy mindset prior to coaching. These might include the following.

- I value myself and my colleagues.
- I believe that:
  - I have perceptions and mindsets that offer my colleagues learning and increased effectiveness;
  - the team and the individuals in it are phenomenally successful when they fully embrace the coaching culture;
  - coaches and coachees both learn from their interaction;
  - I am an effective coach only when I maintain a healthy relationship with the coachee;
  - an effective coach is only a *catalyst* for learning and change, not a *force* for them;
  - the coachee has the resources necessary for learning; and
  - silences belong to the coachee, not the coach.
- I can:
  - offer *choices*, not solutions and not instructions;
  - offer permission to the coachee and myself;
  - offer the coachee my best attention at all times;
  - remain as flexible in my thinking and actions as possible; and
  - check the coachee's commitment and confidence level.

The coaching style has more to it than the basic mindset established above, and I wish to explore some of the statements in more detail for clarity.

Challenges can be uncomfortable for the coachee. Indeed, inventions will need to be challenging and sometimes uncomfortable if any major impact is going to take place. The greatest learning invariably comes after the coachee has been most challenged and is most uncomfortable. While the facilitating methods that are at the heart of coaching are respectful, they are not necessarily comfortable or gently applied. A coach may be quite ferocious in challenging unproductive thinking. As coach, it is important to realise that the coaching interaction must end with no deterioration in the working relationship that you established at the beginning. A key way for the coach to check this is to ask for feedback after the coaching ends with such questions as:

- Was that helpful?
- Can you offer me clues as to how I might have coached you more effectively?

The coachee has the resources necessary for learning

The great thing about this empowering belief is that it frees up the responsibility of the coach to do something to change the coachee. As soon as that happens, the coachee is free from pressure and can work in a safer environment, where the results of coaching are more significant. Pressure is not a good place to be coached from! What we are really saying is that coaching should be need-free. For example, some beliefs that enhance the coach's mindset may include:

- I do not need to get a result from this coaching.
- I do not need to prove anything to myself.
- I do not need to prove anything to my coachee.

The result of this thinking and mindset is that the coach becomes a *catalyst* for learning and change and not a *force* for them. The learning and motivation thus stays with the coachee.

Silences belong to the coachee and not the coach

Mental adjustment and learning take place in silences (unless the coachee has gone to sleep!). The coach needs to stay quiet and relaxed, breathing quietly and easily without embarrassment or need. It may be disappointing, but some of the best work that the coachee will do often happens in this self-reflective silence. Let the coachee decide when the silence needs to end. A good coach will hold silences for many minutes provided the coachee is still mentally processing. If this period of mental processing seems to be broken, the coach is best advised to ask the same question, or make the same challenge as triggered the self-reflective period. In my experience, the second period is typically shorter and invariably results in a very significant outcome – a cathartic leap of perception or understanding that motivates action.

I offer choices, not solutions nor instructions
Phrase your intervention as questions that *increase* choice rather than *reduce* choice. The coach does this by staying nondirective. An example of a directive question is:

'Why not speak to her yourself?'

The less directive equivalent might be:

'Would you like to change anything in the relationship, and if you did, how would that be?'

Another type of limiting, directive question is:

'How do you *feel* about that?'

The coachee's preference at that moment may be a *visual* picture in which *feeling* is absent. It is therefore better to intervene with a question like 'How do you *experience* that?' so that their thinking and experiencing is not sidetracked by semantics.

I offer permission to the coachee and myself
Give yourself permission to set to one side any personal feeling of criticism or failure. For the coach, permission is therefore the freedom to allow the coachee to explore their material. The coach should not get in the way of that.

I offer the coachee my best attention at all times
Attention is probably the greatest gift that any coach offers the coachee. Coachees will invariably arrive at a new perception of their situation if they can talk through things with someone else (whether the coach introduces potential for new thinking or not). Quality attention is need-free attention. Body language should be neutral, and to some extent may match that of the coachee.[16] The coach should be quite relaxed and calm. The physical distance between the coach and the coachee needs to be comfortable for both parties and free of tables and other encumbrances. Ideally, your body direction should not be square-on, as this can feel confrontational. The coach should not nod or offer affirmatives, such as 'that's right', 'yes' and 'I agree'. Habitual affirmations like this can lead to serious complications where they are accepting of a dysfunctional belief, sense of self or behaviour.

Eye contact needs to be good but should not be forced. The coach's speech should be measured and calm. It is a good idea to match the pace of the coachee's speech, except where the coachee is anxious and fast. The coach must not fiddle or look at their watch!

I remain as flexible in my thinking and actions as possible
The coach needs to be able to work with whatever is happening in the moment, free from panic. Giving away responsibility for silences will help in this. The coach's self-trust is also a gift to the coachee. If you are calm and not busy processing irrelevant information internally when the coachee is talking, then you have the best chance of keeping your attention with the coachee and offering new choices. Here is an empowering belief: 'If there is an appropriate intervention, it will arise automatically.'

Where the coachee decides on action, I will check his commitment and his confidence level
I wish to add some words already written about the subject of the criteria for successful commitments and confidence levels. It is a

---

[16] Sometimes a coach will follow a period of matching in order to change the pace, keep interest or alter the energy in the dynamic.

reminder about action and the need to check out the future events (if applicable). For example, let's imagine that James has decided that in future he will ask for meetings and preset agendas with his immediate boss. Up until now he has waited for his boss to set up meetings without knowing why they have been called, and this has made him anxious. He feels that meetings go badly and that he does not come across well. Once James has been coached to this new action, it is valuable to check out a real future event. Use the timeline or ask the coachee to imagine the future event and effectively have an experience of it in the present. This sensory journey is sometimes called *future pacing* (in NLP terms). It is one thing to be confident about a new diet for losing weight. It is entirely another matter to attempt it in real life. Future pacing allows a more real experience of what the future is like *now*, so that any commitment has the highest possible chance of success.

Appendix 4

The Coaching Session

The coaching culture assumes that the coach–coachee relationship happens automatically and spontaneously as needed. Sometimes, where there is an issue raised by a coachee who is looking for coaching, a set time and place may be arranged for coaching. In this situation it is possible to improve the setting and add a little structure to the coaching session in order to improve the quality of the facilitation. My book *Performance Coaching – The Handbook for Managers, HR Professionals and Coaches* (see 'References', page 149) goes into a great deal of detail and offers practical methods for dealing with real issues. Here is an outline of best practice.

Set a time and place. Ideally, let hem know how you coach and give some expectation of what is likely to happen. Arrange for a secure and private room and turn off telephones and other distractions. Make sure that the room feels private and comfortable. Have at least three chairs in the room so that (if necessary) the coachee can physically move to explore different perceptions. The room should be big enough (ideally) to permit a coachee to walk a timeline (if this is useful) during the session. Have a watch or clock where you can both see it without effort. Do not have a table or anything else between you.

Leave the choice of seating to the coachee. In order to do that, make sure that you have not staked a claim to a chair – leave any documents, jacket etc. elsewhere in the room. This process makes a powerful statement: 'I am not your manager in this interaction: I am a servant-leader, here to help you.'[17] This frees up the situation and helps the coachee to go further in their thinking and self-reflection than might otherwise be possible. Ask them if they have any questions about the session and, if rapport seems to be good, ask them if they are ready to start with the coaching.

---

[17] Servant-leadership is a complete discipline initiated by Robert Greenleaf (see, for example, Greenleaf and Spears, 1998).

Establish an objective for the session. Make a reality check to be sure that the objective is reachable within the time set aside for the session. If it is not, limit the objective or ask them to chunk it down to an element that is key. Ask the coachee to affirm that the objective is what he wishes to work on.

Stay with the mindset that you have established prior to the session. Continue to permit yourself to be flexible and open. When you think the session may be complete, check with the coachee that this is their perception also. Check their state. Is the coachee more energetic and enthusiastic than before? If in doubt, ask what difference they experience. And ask for feedback. What could you have done better for that individual coachee?

One of the best ways to learn how to be an excellent coach is to make sure that you are regularly a coachee as well. A number of organisations promote co-coaching, including one of my own, the Coaching Foundation. In addition, there is learning from feedback.

Appendix 5

Prioritisation or Ranking Process

Imagine that there are four actions you need to take. Here they are:

1. Register today to present a paper at the annual company conference.
2. Speak with Susan about our row over Stephen by Friday.
3. Book first driving lesson this evening at seven o'clock.
4. Read through merger files Tuesday morning over breakfast.

Now take the *first two* of your own actions and ask this question: 'If I could do only one of these actions, which is the more important for me to do?'

Using the example above, if the answer Action 2 ('Speak with Susan ...') is more important than Action 1 ('Register today ...'), then write down as here, with Action 2 higher up the list than Action 1 and lots of space for other actions:

Ranking
Action 2. Susan
Action 1. Register today

Now ask the same question about Actions 2 and 3: 'If I could only do one of these actions, which is the more important for me to do?'

If you answer that Action 2 ('Speak with Susan ...) is more important than Action 3 ('Book first driving lesson ...'), then write down as here, placing Action 3 *below* Action 2 but *with* Action 1, since we do not yet know which is more important:

Ranking
Action 2. Susan
Action 3. Book driving lesson
Action 1. Register today

Now ask the same question about Actions 3 and 1: 'If I could do only one of these actions, which is the more important for me to do?'

If you answer that Action 3 ('Book first driving lesson ...') is more important than Action 1 ('Register today ...'), then write down as here:

Ranking
Action 2. Susan
Action 3. Driving lesson at 7 p.m.
Action 1. Register today

To find out whether Action 4 or 2 is more important, ask the same question: 'If I could only do one of these actions, which is the more important for me to do?'

If you answer that Action 4 ('Read through merger files ...') is more important than Action 2 ('Speak with Susan ...'), then write it down as here, with Action 4 higher up the list than Action 2:

Ranking
Action 4. Read merger files Tuesday
Action 2. Susan
Action 3. Driving lesson at 7 p.m.
Action 1. Register today

You should now have a fail-safe ranking for progress. The ranking process is a valuable tool for deciding where to place your energy and action. If you have ranked your own actions, double-check your confidence score (0–10). If it is less than 8 you may need to drop that action or review its importance for you. Remember to let gut feeling influence you.

Glossary

Belief, empowering
An exigent or adopted reality of an individual that encourages new perception and choice.

Belief, limiting
An exigent or adopted reality of an individual that discourages new perception and choice.

Broken-record technique
The use of one or more precise phrases to help diffuse conflict and to keep an argument specific to the context.

Chunking down
The follower's question, 'What stops me?', which is used repeatedly to find the primary obstacle to achieving a specific goal.

Chunking up
The leader's question, 'So what would that do for me?', which is used repeatedly to find the primary motivating experience for driving towards a specific goal.

Coaching
Techniques (in total trust and rapport) that encourage an individual to fresh solutions by stimulating their thinking and experience by the use of challenge (to thinking), questions and silence (creating self-reflection and cathartic change).

Collaboration
Working with another or others to create win–win agreements with a specific goal or goals.

Compromise
Trading with another or others to reach agreements with a specific goal or goals.

Destiny
A belief that there are ideal tasks and goals (in life) that, if recognised, provide the individual with the greatest possible satisfaction and success.

Fate
A belief that everything is preordained.

Feedback
Written (and preferably) face-to-face imparting of constructive criticism/observations/perceptions without value judgment. Ideally, the feedback contains only observable (measurable) facts about behaviours and includes a scenario about the influence that proposed and specific changes in behaviour might make to the individual and those around them.

51 Per Cent Rule
The rule that states that, in any given interaction, I am 51 per cent responsible for the result of that interaction.

Leadership
Motivation by example and/or appeal to purpose, identity, value and beliefs. Leadership involves flexibility to switch from managing to facilitating styles as necessary in any given moment.

Matching and mismatching
The tendency (or otherwise) of an individual (in a given context) to mimic or contrast with the behaviour(s) of another person or group of people.

Mentoring
Techniques that offer choices of methods for solving problems and achieving goals, especially where those choices come from the 'mentor'.

Metaphor
A representation (e.g. story, picture, sound) of anything that can expressed directly in words.

Mindset
A state of mind in which a number of beliefs are exigent (or adopted) that predispose that individual to think and act in a particular way in a given context. Very often a mindset will be influenced by a conscious understanding of values, identity and purpose.

Needs
Fundamental requirements for health and efficacy.

Neuro-linguistic programming
Neuro-linguistic programming (NLP), developed from the ideas of a group of people who wished to explore new perceptions of reality and gain practical methods for helping themselves and others to develop their thinking, wellbeing and success. NLP now embraces many ideas and 'tools' taken or adapted from many other disciplines. These tools are useful in self-development. The best practitioners of NLP are those who do not simply use these tools but have the courage, openness and flexibility to develop themselves using all methods available to them. Four areas of competence underpin NLP (see 'Rapport', page 148).

Outcome
Desired result.

Patterns
Repeated episodes of thinking processes or behaviours.

Perceptual positions
The first perceptual position is a person's state of being when they are fully associated mentally with their sensing of themselves and their reality of the world (real or imagined) around them. The second and third positions are 'virtual states' of mind in which the person mentally adopts the perceived world of others. The second position is the adoption of the perceived state of another specific individual for the purpose of learning. The third position (a dissociated state) is the adoption of the state of an imaginary 'observer'. Other perceptual positions are also virtual states and can include the 'higher self' or 'shadow self', for example.

Performance mindsets
Thinking strategies for individual and Team performance (see, also, 'Mindset', page 147).

Rapport
One of the four pillars that underpin neuro-linguistic programming (NLP). Rapport is a measure of the quality of the dynamic in a relationship, especially in regard to confidentiality, trust, openness and listening/communication skills. The other three pillars are flexibility, sensory acuity and outcome thinking.

Reframing
To reframe an idea, communication or situation means to look openly for other possible meanings and perspectives for the purpose of learning.

Sensory journey
Method of richly experiencing the future as if it were happening now.

Team
Any group of people working collectively towards a shared goal or purpose.

Values
Those fundamental qualities that are held most precious by an individual or group.

Wants
Simple desires that may or may not be realistic. Realistic 'wants' are often used as rewards.

Win–win
Situation in which all the individuals/parties gain from the agreement or arrangement.

References

Bateson, G (1972) *Steps to an Ecology of Mind* (New York, NY: Ballantine).

Buzan, T (2006) *The Ultimate Book of Mind Maps* (London: Harper Thorsons).

Charvet, S (1997) *Words That Change Minds* (2nd edn) (Dubuque, Iowa: Kendall Hunt).

Dilts, R (1994) *Strategy of Genius*, Vol. I (Boulder, CO: Paladin Press).

Erdmann, E, Hubel, D H, and Stover, D (2000) *Beyond a Wall Divided: Human Values in the Brain-Mind Science of Roger Sperry* (Lincoln, NEAuthors Choice Press).

Gallwey, W T (2000), *The Inner Game of Work* (New York, NY, and Toronto: Random House).

Greenleaf, R K, and Spears, L (2001) 'Power of Servant Leadership', in L C Spears, and M Lawrence (eds), *Focus on Leadership: Servant Leadership for the 21st Century* (New York, NY: John Wiley).

Hall, L M, and Bodenhamer, B (1997) *Time-Lining* (Carmarthen, Wales: Crown House Publishing).

Harris, T (1973) *I'm Okay, You're Okay* (London: Pan).

McLeod, A (2003) *Performance Coaching – The Handbook for Managers, HR Professionals and Coaches* (Carmarthen, Wales: Crown House).

McLeod, A (2007) *From Manager to Leader: Self-Coaching Personal Performance* (forthcoming).

McLeod, A, *Slay that Dragon* (forthcoming).

Pritchard, J (1997) 'Diagnosing Conflict Within Joint Ventures and Alliances', *Rapport* 36, pp. 3–5.

Index

*Note: **Bold type** indicates key references.*

Index of exercises